Breakthrough Astrology Series

Astrology For The Absolute Beginner

by Mark Mann

How To Interpret Your Own Birth Chart
Volume I

The Meaning of Astrological Symbolism
Signs   Houses   Planets
Your Personal Journal and Workbook

Breakthrough Enterprises
P.O. Box 5511
Eugene, Oregon 97405

Meaning of logo (designed by Katherine Deal):

My natal Sun is in Aries 5 degrees. The Sabian symbol for this degree is ''A Triangle with Wings.''

In Dane Rudhyar's book, An Astrological Mandala, his description of the meaning of this symbol includes the following:

Keynote: The capacity for self-transcending...A NEW DIMENSION of being is envisioned mobilizing creative endeavors.

My natal Moon is in Leo and my rising sign is in Sagittariuis; therefore I included the symbols for Aries, Leo and Sagittarius (a fire trine) on the three points of the triangle.

Quotes on pages 11, 19, and 23 are from Dane Rudhyar, The Astrology of Personality, Aurora Press, 1991.

Cover Deisgn Concept: Katy Keuter
Design and Production: Beneda Design

Published by:
American Federation of Astrologers, Inc.
PO Box 22040
6535 S. Rural Road
Tempe, AZ 85285-2040

Printed in the United States of America

This book is dedicated to my partner, Diana, who has given me her emotional support as well as her precious time and wisdom during my writing and revising of this book; to our children and grandchildren for being sources of inspiration; and to my mother who has provided me with continuing encouragement in my creative pursuits.

Table Of Contents

Preface

Astrology is one method of becoming aware of the practical and far-reaching wisdom found in the cyclical patterns of life. The more aware you are of these amazing patterns, the more you will be able to understand how to creatively use your imagination, intuition and assertiveness to bring new potentials of yourself into reality. This workbook gives you the first steps towards discovering your unique potentials and path in life through the interpretation of your birth chart.

A 29-year-old of female client of mine who lives in another city once wrote the following to me in a letter:

"I want to continue to discover new purposes and meaning for myself. I try to make the best decisions I can about my career, making a decent income, being responsive to my husband and children, doing my part to help make the world a better place to live, and so on. But sometimes I've wished, I had a compass or a map, something to guide me. I survive well enough day-to-day, and I generally feel good about myself and my family. Yet at times I wish I had more insight into what my purposes in life might be. In talking with a friend recently I learned astrology can provide not only this guidance, it can also describe how complex I feel I really am. I'm curious and ready to learn what I may not already know about myself in order to continue growing."

The desire to become more conscious of our unique potentials is a powerful need felt by everyone at some time. This book has been written to aid you in your search. It allows you to use astrology as a tool for self-discovery and self-actualization.

There is a profound difference between the "Sun Sign" astrology found in newspapers and magazines and the serious study of astrology. During the twentieth century astrology has become a popular form of entertainment. As a matter of fact, 'astrologer' is listed in the **US Dictionary of Occupational Titles** as an entertainer. While this "fortune-telling" aspect of astrology has provided fun and entertainment for many people, it has been at the expense of the deeper value it can have for everyone.

Astrology is increasingly being used by people who are continuing to pursue their psychological and spiritual development and self-actualization. The reason why astrology is so useful in this respect is that in its purest sense it is all-inclusive and not prejudiced by cultural, political psychological or religious biases. It is an extremely comprehensive life model in which all parts of life have their place, and it is a model that allows you to understand how all the different sides of life and your psychological nature can relate to each other in the most effective ways. Astrological insights can enhance and be applied to any personal, psychological, religious or political or belief.

The basic principles of astrology can be easily learned. You do not have to learn a lot of confusing jargon to be able to gain valuable insights into your psychological nature and potentials.

Astrology is simply the study of cycles of nature and how cycles give structure and meaning to your life. Once you understand this **cyclical pattern** in terms of **human development** you will be able to use this knowledge to interpret your birth chart. You will be able to use your birth chart to understand the unique path you can take as you develop your potentials.

I wrote this book for the general public. Regardless of a person's cultural or religious perspective, I believe that astrology can be both a **practically useful** and a **psychologically meaningful** tool for everyone. It can assist people who want to make conscious choices about how they want to develop themselves, their meaningful relationships, and their relationship to all other aspects of life (career, home, self-expression, social causes, spirituality, etc.).

What Do You Need To Be Able To Use This Book?

You do not need to know anything about astrology to be able to use this book. It is written to allow a person with no background in astrology to be able to interpret his or her chart.

You will need your birth chart to be able to complete the exercises that come later in the book. Possible avenues to purchase a computer generated chart can be found in Appendix I. The cost is approximately $5.

On the opposite page is a diagram of a computerized chart.

DON'T WORRY ABOUT ALL OF THE SYMBOLS AND NUMBERS ON THE DIAGRAM. YOU DO NOT NEED TO KNOW WHAT MOST OF THESE SYMBOLS MEAN TO BEGIN INTERPRETING YOUR BIRTH CHART WITH THIS BOOK.

In the first section of this book I teach you how to read the symbols you need to know in the chart. Then I teach you the meanings of the basic astrological symbolism in both cyclical and psychological terms. Next I provide easy-to-use exercises that will allow you to begin interpreting your chart.

You need to know that you will have many questions at the beginning. You will be facing ideas that may seem ambiguous or contradictory. However, you

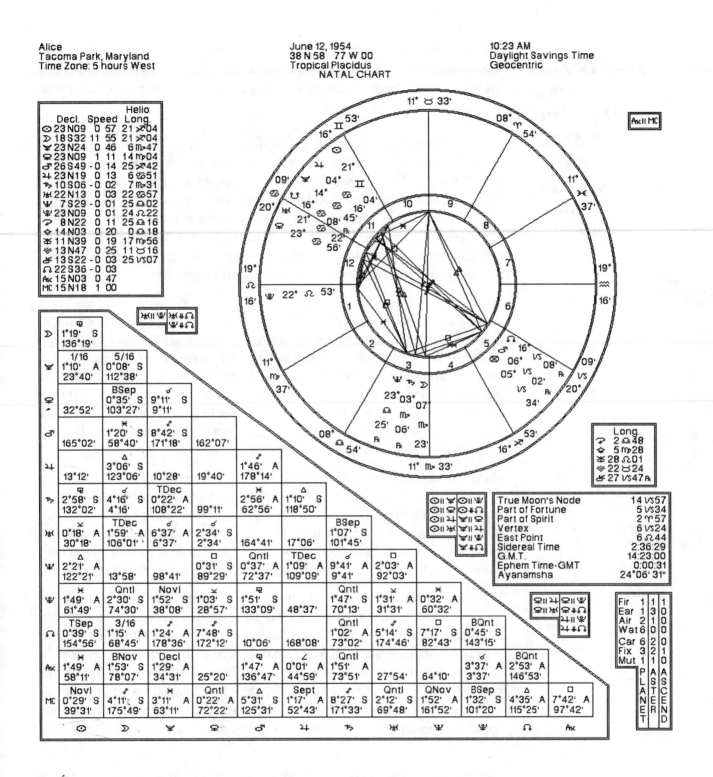

Alice
Tacoma Park, Maryland
Time Zone: 5 hours West

June 12, 1954
38 N 58   77 W 00
Tropical Placidus
NATAL CHART

10:23 AM
Daylight Savings Time
Geocentric

will have many opportunities to explore the answers to your questions as you continue through the book.

How Is This Book Different than Many Other Beginning Astrology Books?

A good friend of mine who has never used or studied astrology recently asked me how he could begin to study astrology if he wanted to objectively determine its validity.

I asked him why he would want to determine astrology's validity. He answered that it was because a number of people whom he knows and respects, such as myself, use astrology. He said lately he had been thinking that perhaps it might be a blind spot in him that didn't allow him to take the time to investigate the validity of astrology for himself. He said that he wanted to find out what astrology could offer him, but that he didn't know where to start. He said that one day he went into a bookstore with a large astrology section, and looked through some of the books but couldn't find the right one.

My friend's dilemma is common. During the last 25 years many excellent astrological books have been written, translating astrological symbolism into modern concepts and applications. However, most of these books require you to already know something about astrology. Most of these books do not provide you, an **absolute beginner**, clear and simple explanations of how the astrological symbolism derives its meaning. Finally most of these books do not provide you with a process to follow in order to learn how to translate the astrological symbolism of your birth chart into everyday language that will individually and specifically mean something to you.

Many introductory books on astrology offer definitions for the basic symbolism of astrology without telling you how these definitions have been determined. If you are going to be able to use astrology in a personal and practical way, you have to understand the interconnective patterns behind the symbolism. If you are truly going to learn to "think astrologically," you have to understand how the pattern of cyclical development applies to human behavior and potential.

If a writer tells you what a sign or house means without telling you how that meaning has been derived, you have not been given the necessary knowledge to make your own interpretations. Why is Aries associated with assertiveness? Why is Cancer associated with emotional sensitivity? Isn't Pisces also associated with emotional sensitivity? What is the difference between the emotional sensitivity of Cancer and of Pisces? Why does Mercury symbolize our rational mind and Jupiter our abstract mind? Why does the 7th House symbolize general social relationships and the 8th House symbolize intimate one-to-one emotional sharing?

One purpose of this book is to explain how the basic symbolism of astrology is based upon the cyclical development of energy. Another purpose is to give you the ability to translate astrological terminology and symbolism into ideas that you can understand and apply to your personal development.

It's difficult to imagine a building contractor being able to construct a new building without blueprints that show how all the various parts of the building interconnect. Based upon this blueprint the contractor is able to schedule the work of plumbers, the electricians, painters, etc. With the blueprint, the contractor can also evaluate if the parts of the building are being constructed in the most effective manner.

A mechanic may be able to fix an automobile engine without having seen a diagrammed model of that particular engine, but if the mechanic had such a model showing the structure of the engine, he/she would be more efficient not only in repairing the engine but in preventing breakdowns.

A good life model should allow us to identify where any one part of life fits into the whole and how these parts relate to one another in a meaningful order. It should also allow us to understand how parts of the whole can work effectively to achieve balance and harmony; thereby, enhancing the parts as well as the whole. I am referring to the whole of an individual's psychological life: **personal, social, and transpersonal.**

The **personal side** of life is experienced by the individual through such ways as being assertive, developing self-reliance, establishing personal resources and financial stability, developing one's mental abilities, and establishing emotional security and a home.

The **social side** of life is experienced by the individual in one-to-one relationships. This side of life is experienced as we develop the ability to play and to work with others, the ability to express ourselves confidently and creatively to others, as well as to serve willingly and help others in useful ways. The social side of life also involves developing intimate unions and being able to share deeply and emotionally with another person.

The **transpersonal side** of life is beyond the personal and interpersonal (social) sides. The transpersonal side of life is experienced by the individual through such ways as meeting community responsibilities, achieving career goals, taking part in group or political activities, searching for and exchanging knowledge and belief systems with others, and being receptive to spiritual realities.

Astrology allows us to explore how we are relating to these various sides of life. Being able to see how all the parts and sides of life and human nature fit together into a meaningful whole encourage understanding and respect, not only for our own, but also for others' beliefs and perspectives. In life, people tend to gravitate to viewpoints or perspectives that include only a few sides of life while excluding and even denouncing other sides of life. This tendency to value **parts** of life rather than the **whole** of life leads to cultural, political, ecological, religious, and racial intolerance and imbalance. A negative imbalance occurs when one side of anything is emphasized at the expense of the other. This imbalance, extremism or bias ultimately leads us to ineffective actions, and at worst to one side turning against another, with destructive results.

Men and women of wisdom throughout human existence have recognized the value of studying cyclical life patterns. These cyclical patterns are reflected in all aspects of life and cultural activities: electrical wave patterns, neurological and cardiovascular patterns, the day and night, the seasons, economic cycles, and so on.

In psychological terms, the value of studying the cyclical process is that it shows not only how the different sides of life relate meaningfully to one another, it also helps us understand how these relationships develop in a way that can be understood and used to enhance self-awareness.

Life provides us with times of obvious opportunities as well as traumas. Often we allow these periods to pass without knowing how to use them . . . Traumas and opportunities offer chances to develop different ways of being and understanding. They offer special times to develop our potentials.

Opportunities occur in everyone's life. However, to take full advantage of them, you have to be ready. To be ready you may be required to develop further something inside yourself.

For example, you may receive a large sum of money but if you have not developed financial awareness and skills you may waste it.

You may become aware of an opening for a job that you've always wanted but you must have developed the necessary skills to perform the job successfully.

Traumas can signal the need for change and bring opportunities for further self-actualization. For instance, the loss of a relationship due to self-centeredness on your part may challenge you to develop your abilities to be responsive to the needs of a loved one and to share yourself more fully in an intimate relationship. A job loss may force you to develop new work skills. The death of a loved one may help you recognize your need to develop a sense of inner security, and allow you to develop a fuller spiritual life.

In 1987 I was involved in a highly unusual and near fatal automobile accident (for those of you who know astrology, I had Uranus transiting my ascendant). I was driving a colleague's 1986 Honda Accord 65 mph north on a freeway. A semi-truck with two trailers driving in the southbound lane suddenly lost control and headed across the grassy meridian directly in front of my car. Tall bushes had blocked my view of the truck until it shot out in front of me. I had no opportunity to stop or even swerve. I don't remember the impact of the crash but our car miraculously entered the space between the front and back wheels of the second trailer, passing underneath between this narrow space. The roof was torn off the top of the car and my left ear almost off my head. My ear required relatively minor reconstruction that left barely perceptible scars.

I was extremely fortunate to be alive. The result and great benefit of this traumatic accident was that it forced me to reevaluate certain aspects of my life. My life had become highly fast-paced and single-focused at the expense of maintaining a more balanced life style. The accident had the effect of shattering my narrow focus and challenging me to slow down. My birth chart indicates that I have an ability to coordinate many projects and respond to many demands at once. However, I had allowed myself to become overextended, working long hours and even weekends. The accident forced me to stop everything. With time to reflect it became clear I had allowed the goals I was pursuing to blind me to other needs and areas of my life. I returned to my birth chart in order to regain the perspective I needed to bring my lifestyle into more balance.

All of your experiences as well as your responses to them can be studied in terms of the cyclical life patterns depicted in your birth chart. This means that you can study your birth chart to gain insight about the skills and qualities you are naturally inclined to develop. You can be aware or unaware of your inclinations but, regardless, you will seek experiences that challenge you to develop your unique potentials.

Astrology can help us with these key experiences in life by giving us a symbolic tool to use in order to understand the meaning cycles and phases of cycles have in our lives. Understanding astrology offers us access to a comprehensive psychological life model of human developmental potentials.

A Challenge To The Skeptical Reader: Be Open And Judge For Yourself

"How are discoveries made in modern physics? The classical explanation is that a physicist observes a fact which is new, or ponders upon some flaw in an old theory, and formulates a new hypothesis which explains the new fact or solves the old unsolved enigma. The hypothesis is then checked by testing all the possible consequences thereof; and it becomes accepted theory if it fits in with every known fact and is invalidated by none. We might assume that astrology originated in a similar manner. Some striking event coincided with a planetary conjunction*. The hypothesis that both were related arose in the mind of the observer, who checked it with similar occurrences — and after a few generations of checking up, this conjunction was definitely considered to bring about a certain event, or at least a type of event."

Dane Rudyar from *The Astrology of Personality*

* Conjunction: two or more planets in the same or near the same position in relation to the cycle of the zodiacal signs.

Our modern scientifically based society is obsessed with defining reality only by what it can prove with scientific research. Yet scientific perception has its own limitations. It can prove or disprove only what it can see or measure. Science is continually discovering new laws and realities of which it has not previously been aware. For example, in 1979 the Voyager space probe allowed us to see that Jupiter has three more moons circling around it than could previously be seen from earth. Everyone is familiar with Einstein's astounding revelations earlier in this century on the nature of energy. However, for over two thousand years metaphysical disciplines such as astrology have been based on these same principles of energy that the modern physicists have only recently recognized.

Science measures the cyclical processes of energy while astrology describes how these cyclical processes of energy can have meaning for us in our daily lives. During the last fifty or sixty years astrological symbols representing these cyclical patterns have been translated into psychological terms by astrologers. This book explains how the astrological symbolism relates to a comprehensive psychological model of life, and will give you the means to objectively apply the symbolism to analyze your own birth chart.

Whether or not you believe astrology works, I hope the most skeptical reader will take the time to study his or her own birth chart objectively and openly. For only at this point will readers be able to judge whether or not astrology is valid for them.

A Suggestion To The Reader

This book is not meant to be read cover to cover in a few sittings. You need to give yourself time to reflect on the meanings of the symbolism of your birth chart.

I know life is busy today and we often do not have the time and energy to tackle such complex subjects as astrology. However, the study of astrology becomes exciting when you use it to learn more about yourself. As a tool, astrology allows you to shape your future, create your own life story.

Once you understand how to use the exercises in this book, you will be able to use it even if you just have a few minutes. If you have a few minutes one day, you can complete the blanks of one of the sentences. After completing the blanks, you will begin to see the meaning of a planet's signs and house positions. Perhaps a few days later, you will have the time to return to the book and write about what the sentence and symbolism may mean for you. You may stay with this sentence for a few weeks or longer before you go on to the next sentence. An important point is that you can choose to go back many times to the exercises to reaffirm insights and/or to gain new meaning.

Determine Signs
And House Positions
In Your Birth Chart

In this chapter you will learn:

1. The symbols for planets, signs and houses.

2. How to refer to these symbols to determine the signs and house positions of the planets in your birth chart.

On these two pages you can see the symbols for the planets, signs and houses. You are not being asked to do anything with these symbols yet. On the following pages I have provided instructions to help you refer to these symbols as you determine the signs and house positions of the planets in your birth chart.

Later when using the exercises in Chapters Four and Six, you will need to know your planets' signs and house positions in order to begin to interpret their meanings.

Planets

Definition: **Planets** symbolize ten basic Psychological Functions or capacities in the human psyche. (The Sun and Moon are considered planets from earths perspective.)

Symbols For The Planets:

☉	Sun	♂	Mars	♆	Neptune
☽	Moon	♃	Jupiter	♀	Pluto
☿	Mercury	♄	Saturn		
♀	Venus	♅	Uranus		

Signs

Definition: **Signs** symbolize twelve **Ways Of Being Or Acting**. The signs symbolize twelve basic characteristics of human behavior.

♈	Aries	♌	Leo	♐	Sagittarius
♉	Taurus	♍	Virgo	♑	Capricorn
♊	Gemini	♎	Libra	♒	Aquarius
♋	Cancer	♏	Scorpio	♓	Pisces

Houses

Definition: **Houses** symbolize twelve **Focuses Of Activities** in life. The houses symbolize twelve basic experiences in human life.

Birth Chart Diagram for the Houses:

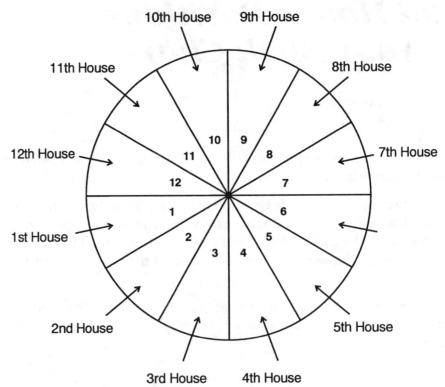

figure 1

Note: In Chapter Three the meanings of the signs, houses, and planets are defined with an in-depth explanation of how these meanings have been determined.

Determining Your Sign And House Positions

Before searching for the symbols of the signs and house positions of the planets in your birth chart, let's look at these symbols in Alice's chart (page 7). This will help orient you to their placement in a birth chart.

First, let's look at the symbols for the planets in her birth chart:

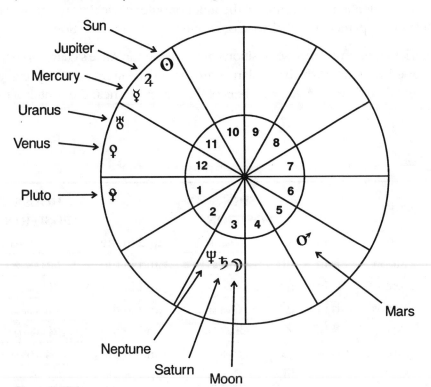

figure 2

Note: Some of the symbols for planets in Alice's computerized chart are written near the outer circle (☉♃☿♅♀♀), while others are written near the center (♆♄☽ ♂). In every birth chart diagram, the planets' symbols are written inside the outer circle. However, it is the choice of the person diagramming the birth chart whether a planet's symbol is written near the outer or inner circle.

Next, let's look at the planets next to the symbols for their sign positions in her birth chart:

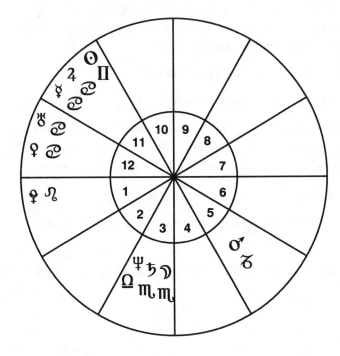

figure 3

Note: The symbol for the sign is written on either side of the planet it describes. It may be written in the direction of the inner or outer circle. It is not shown to the side of the planet in a clockwise or counter-clockwise direction.

Finally, let's identify the house positions of the planets in Alice's chart. Note the pie-shaped sections in which the planets are located in Figure 2 on the previous page, and then determine the numbers of these sections near the center of the circle.

Signs And House Positions In Alice's Birth Chart

PLANET			SIGN POSITION			HOUSE POSITION
☉	Sun	is in	♊	Gemini	and in the	11th House
☽	Moon	is in	♏	Scorpio	and in the	3rd House
☿	Mercury	is in	♋	Cancer	and in the	11th House
♀	Venus	is in	♋	Cancer	and in the	12th House
♂	Mars	is in	♑	Capricorn	and in the	5th House
♃	Jupiter	is in	♋	Cancer	and in the	11th House
♄	Saturn	is in	♏	Scorpio	and in the	3rd House
♅	Uranus	is in	♋	Cancer	and in the	12th House
♆	Neptune	is in	♎	Libra	and in the	3rd House
♇	Pluto	is in	♌	Leo	and in the	1st House

Now you can use the following steps to determine the signs and house positions of the planets in your birth chart. Remember at this time you will only be using the symbols for the planets, signs and houses. You do not have to know the meanings or significance of any other numbers or symbols.

Write your signs and house positions in the appropriate blanks on the next page. Again, you need to know these positions in order to begin your interpretation using the exercises in later sections.

Step 1: Locate the symbol for your Sun (☉).

Step 2: Determine the sign position of the Sun.

Remember that the symbol for the sign is written next to the planet's symbol in the direction of the inner or outer circle. Write the symbol and the name of your Sun's sign position in the appropriate blank on the next page.

Step 3: Determine the house position of the Sun.

Remember that you are identifying the number of the pie-shaped segment in which the Sun is located.

Write the number of your Sun's house position in the appropriate blank on the next page.

Step 4: Determine the sign position and house positions for the rest of your planets and write them in the appropriate blanks below.

PLANET		SIGN POSITION		HOUSE POSITION
☉	Sun	is in _____	and in the	_____
☽	Moon	is in _____	and in the	_____
☿	Mercury	is in _____	and in the	_____
♀	Venus	is in _____	and in the	_____
♂	Mars	is in _____	and in the	_____
♃	Jupiter	is in _____	and in the	_____
♄	Saturn	is in _____	and in the	_____
♅	Uranus	is in _____	and in the	_____
♆	Neptune	is in _____	and in the	_____
♇	Pluto	is in _____	and in the	_____

Signs And House Positions Of The Planets In Your Birth Chart

Appendix II, How to Read Your Birth Chart Form, provides further discussions on how the planets, signs and houses are represented in the birth chart.

In the next two chapters I explain the psychological concepts and astrological symbolism that you need to know to use the interpretive exercise provided you later in the book.

Understanding Your Birth Chart In Terms of Psychological Potentials

What we vaguely and confusingly call "destiny" is simply the process of actualization of the potentialities abstractly formulated in the birth-chart . . .

. . . the purpose of this astro-psychology is to help the person actualize this innate potential, to bring what is only possible to at least a relatively complete state of fulfillment . . .

. . . Selfhood progresses by fulfillment of moments; and each moment or cycle presents us with a new quality which is to be fulfilled . . . the function of astrology is not to tell us what will, or rather may, happen in the future, but what significance there is in every moment or cycle lived or about to be lived. It reveals the quality of particular moments and the larger cycles rooted in those moments. . .

. . . We therefore face the human being through his birth-chart mostly as a psychological entity. He is a particular, unique being. There is no other being exactly like him. Yet we realize also that this unique being is a compound of elements which are not only found in him, but in the multitude of other beings. . .

from Dane Rudyar, *The Astrology of Personality.*

Within each person exists an innate psychological drive for self-actualization. When I use the term, "self-actualization," I am referring to the inner urge each of us has to develop our individual potentials and to achieve our goals and purposes in life.

Your purposes may be varied. You might seek to fully express your love to someone else, to establish a successful business, to climb a mountain, to be artistic, to solve a complex mental problem, to create and maintain a garden, to invest money to make more money, to help others in a community services project, to simply feel fulfilled and satisfied.

Understanding your unique potentials is the first step in your process of self-actualization. As you learn the universal patterns on which astrological symbolism is based, you will also learn how to apply these patterns and symbolism to assist you in a goal of psychological development and enhancement.

In the first few pages of this book you have read that astrology studies how cyclical patterns of life apply to human behavior and potential. Before we study the cyclical symbolism of astrology it is important that you understand what I mean by the psychological terms I will be using.

Psychology

Psychology refers to the study of an individual's conscious and unconscious perceptions, responses and behaviors involving all sides of life: personal, social, transpersonal (community and spiritual).

The goals of astrology as applied to psychology are to assist you:

- to identify all the parts of yourself (your psyche) and to integrate them consciously in your individuality.

- to understand your unique potentials.

- to develop and actualize your unique potentials.

Individuality

Your individuality is the totality of your self: who you are, who you are becoming and who you can be. Your individuality consists of your potential for uniqueness as you consciously develop all sides of yourself.

Personality

The term personality is the outward expression of your psychological nature and individuality. It is how you appear to others on a day-to-day basis as you express yourself mentally, emotionally through many types of behavior. However, how you appear to others at any given time will not be all that there is to your individuality.

The term, psyche, refers to your inner nature. Your inner nature consists of:

Psyche

- Innate (inborn) characteristics, urges, tendencies and potentials.

- Psychological functions that carry out behaviors and responses to life experiences.

- Conscious thoughts, emotions and memories.

- Unconscious mental and emotional processes.

Within your psyche exists the urge for you to become aware of and develop all sides of your inner nature.

Astrology allows you to study your psyche and understand how its various psychological functions enable you to perceive and respond to life's opportunities and challenges.

Psychological functions are the parts of your psyche that allow you to behave and respond to life in different ways. Psychological functions translate your inner urges and tendencies into behavior and responses to life.

Psychological Functions

Astrology allows us to see that the psyche is made up of at least ten different psychological functions. One psychological function allows us to think rationally (symbolized by Mercury). Another allows us to respond to others emotionally (symbolized by the Moon). Another allows us to think abstractly (symbolized by Jupiter). Another allows us to act with personal willpower (symbolized by Mars). Some of these psychological functions allow us to perceive the world consciously (Mercury and Jupiter). Others relate more to unconscious functions (Uranus, Neptune, Pluto). In the next section I will define these main psychological functions of the psyche that astrology symbolizes in more detail.

The different psychological functions of your psyche are constantly evolving through phases of cyclical development. This means that you have the potential to continually become more adept and more refined in your behavior and responses to life: your thinking, expressing your feelings, communicating and so on.

Developmental Potentials

The birth chart symbolizes what specific behaviors, characteristics and psychological functions you are naturally inclined to develop and use as you express your individuality. Therefore, I refer to these natural inclinations as your developmental potentials.

Psychological Development

Psychological development refers to the cyclical processes by which you actualize your innate potentials; the cyclical processes by which you become self-actualized. These psychological processes involve consciously bringing into day-to-day reality the behavior, skills, and characteristics which are your developmental potentials.

In the following section I will explain more specifically how the concepts of psychological development and developmental potentials relate to the astrological symbolism of signs, houses and planets.

I will also be explaining how the cycle, as the main underlying principle of astrological symbolism, gives us a psychological model by which to organize life experiences in developmental terms.

By understanding this basis of astrological symbolism you will be able to discover your own unique developmental potentials using the astrological symbolism of your birth chart.

The Basic Symbolism
Of Astrology
and The Cyclical
Development Of Energy

Section 1... "Life is Cyclical Motion."

Astrology is the study of human behavior and potential in terms of cycles of energy. The term "energy" refers to the basic qualities of force and activity that give structure and meaning to all forms and processes in our time-space dimension.

The common pattern of all energy activity is the cycle. Energy takes on different qualities depending on its phase of development in a cycle.

It means one thing if a form of energy, such as a human being, a plant, a creative expression or a psychological process is in its first stages of development in a particular cycle; it means something quite different if an energy form is in its middle, or last stage of development.

In the cycle of the seasons, spring means something different than fall; in the cycle of the day, sunrise has qualities different from those of sunset. Individuals born in particular phases of these universal cycles reflect the qualities of these phases.

The cycle of the seasons and the cycle of the day symbolize the basic astrological frameworks that give meaning to our psychological functions and daily existence:

from The Astrology of Personality, Dane Rudhyar

The Cycle of the Seasons: (tropical zodiacal cycle)

Cycle of the Seasons

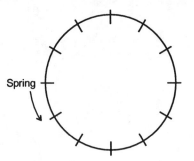

figure 4

The Cycle of the Day: (earth's rotation)

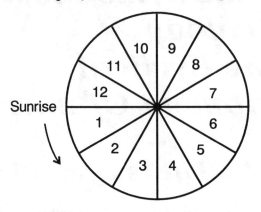

figure 5

The key astrological symbols — **Signs, Houses, Planets** — derive their meaning from the **DEVELOPMENTAL PHASES** of these cycles. All cycles exhibit a common process of development. The first step in understanding astrological symbolism therefore is to understand how energy develops through phases of a cycle.

Section 2...Developmental Phases Of A Cycle

As energy proceeds through a cycle it follows a common pattern. This pattern is based on dividing the cycle into phases of development. Studying how energy changes as it evolves, or moves through the phases of a cycle, can allow us to recognize a common developmental order in life.

Human societies have always divided cycles into phases to give structure and meaning to their lives. The two most common cycles that give structure and meaning of our lives are the Cycle of the Day and the Cycle of the Seasons. In terms of time, the Cycle of the Day is divided into hours, minutes and seconds. Each hour can be thought of as a phase of time, as can each minute and second. In the Cycle of the Seasons, each month can be thought of as a phase. We will return to these two cycles later to see how the signs and house of astrology have derived their meanings from them.

First, it is necessary that you understand the universal pattern that energy follows as it develops through the phases of a cycle, any cycle. Our emphasis here is on understanding the pattern. Next we will relate this cyclical pattern to the astro-psychological model of human development and behavior.

The Cyclical Development of Energy

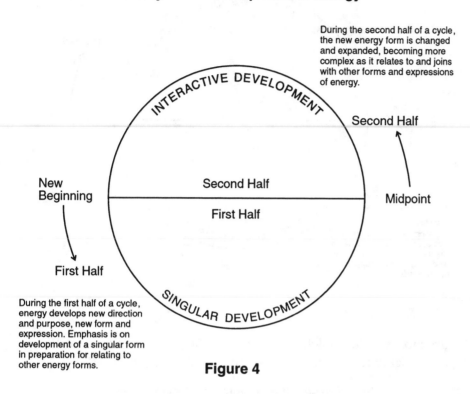

During the second half of a cycle, the new energy form is changed and expanded, becoming more complex as it relates to and joins with other forms and expressions of energy.

During the first half of a cycle, energy develops new direction and purpose, new form and expression. Emphasis is on development of a singular form in preparation for relating to other energy forms.

Figure 4

figure 6

The Phase Of Singular Development

At the beginning of any cycle, energy is projected into a new direction, toward a new purpose, yet it takes the first half of the cycle for this new direction and purpose to become defined, stabilized and perfected.

The Phase Of Interactive Development

At the midpoint, energy is halfway through its cycle and reaches an important turning point. Visually, in the diagram below, you can see that a phase of development has been reached where it is opposite its beginning. This visual representation of opposition symbolizes a stage of development has been reached where the new energy form begins to relate to other energy forms and through such relating is changed. As energy evolves through the second half of the cycle its purpose and direction become more complex. The new energy form is now transformed as a result of relating, sharing and uniting with other energy forms.

This universal pattern of energy as it develops through the cycle can be applied to *two main phases* of psychological development:

Two Phases of Psychological Development

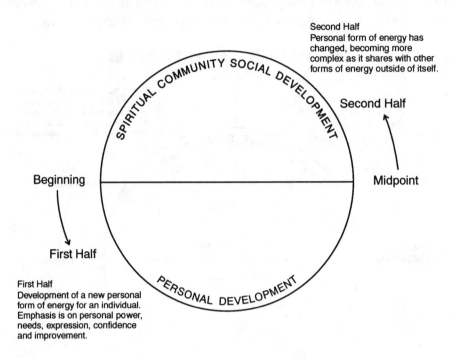

Second Half
Personal form of energy has changed, becoming more complex as it shares with other forms of energy outside of itself.

Second Half

Midpoint

Beginning

First Half

First Half
Development of a new personal form of energy for an individual. Emphasis is on personal power, needs, expression, confidence and improvement.

figure 7

To give more specific or defined meaning to the phase development of energy in psychological terms, we can divide the cycle into *four phases:*

Four Phases of Psychological Development

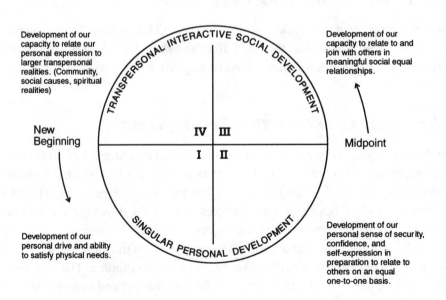

Development of our capacity to relate our personal expression to larger transpersonal realities. (Community, social causes, spiritual realities)

Development of our capacity to relate to and join with others in meaningful social equal relationships.

New Beginning

Midpoint

Development of our personal drive and ability to satisfy physical needs.

Development of our personal sense of security, confidence, and self-expression in preparation to relate to others on an equal one-to-one basis.

figure 8

Analyzing energy as it evolves through *twelve phases* provides us with an even more specific, comprehensive psychological model of human needs and behavior:

Twelve Developmental Phases:

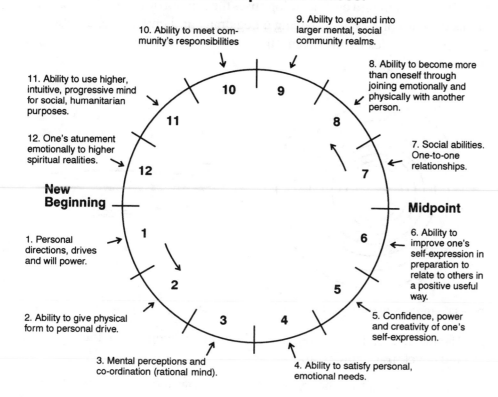

9. Ability to expand into larger mental, social community realms.

10. Ability to meet community's responsibilities

8. Ability to become more than oneself through joining emotionally and physically with another person.

11. Ability to use higher, intuitive, progressive mind for social, humanitarian purposes.

7. Social abilities. One-to-one relationships.

12. One's atunement emotionally to higher spiritual realities.

New Beginning

Midpoint

1. Personal directions, drives and will power.

6. Ability to improve one's self-expression in preparation to relate to others in a positive useful way.

2. Ability to give physical form to personal drive.

5. Confidence, power and creativity of one's self-expression.

3. Mental perceptions and co-ordination (rational mind).

4. Ability to satisfy personal, emotional needs.

figure 9

NOTE: It is beyond the scope of this book to discuss why the cycle is divided into twelve divisions. This topic relates to the metaphysical meaning of numbers and would be better explored at a later stage of study.

We will see in the following sections of this chapter how these twelve different phases define twelve different psychological qualities that are expressed as ways of acting (signs) and focuses of activities (houses).

All cycles follow this order. For example, the cycle of the season begins in the spring when flowers bloom. The day becomes longer than the night. People generally experience a rebirth of energy. New seeds are planted in the earth. These seeds are then harvested during the last part of summer, right before the midpoint of the cycle of the seasons. During the fall equinox the night becomes longer than the day. It's a time when people begin to come indoors and celebrate the culmination of their efforts through social activities. During the winter months it seems as though many plants die back and animals hibernate, waiting for a rebirth in the spring.

The cycle of the day begins at sunrise, the natural time of waking. Usually during the day the individual must perform his work duties, and then in the early evening social relating becomes the important focus. Then individuals go to sleep in preparation for a rebirth at sunrise.

Note: In diagramming a cycle astrology uses the symbol of a circle. Do not think of this diagram of a cycle as having a beginning and end in total isolation of other cycles. Cycles evolve from other cycles and evolve into other cycles (Figure 10).

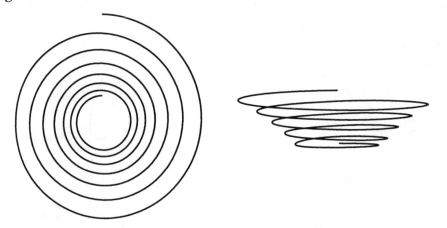

figure 10

This is what we have explored:

1. The first half of the cycle represents how a new energy form is established and develops (Figures 6 and 7).

2. The second half of the cycle represents how the new energy form is transformed and transforms other energy forms through creative interactions and unions (Figures 6 and 7).

3. Cycles can be divided into four main phases (Figure 6). In the cycle of the seasons, the beginnings of these four phases are the spring equinox (March), the summer solstice (June), the fall equinox (September), and the winter equinox (December); and in the cycle of the day the phases are sunrise, noon, sunset and midnight.

4. The main cycles are further divided into twelve phases which can represent twelve developmental phases of human psychological behavior and activities (Figure 9).

Section 3...The Cycle of the Seasons

The seasonal cycle with its interplay of day and night symbolizes the human drama in terms of psychological tendencies to behave in certain ways. The twelve different phases represent twelve different psychological qualities translated into ways of acting.

The cycle of the seasons is the cycle of the year as the earth travels around the sun altering the relationship between day and night. In astrological symbolism the day is seen to represent our individuality, while night represents our ability to interact and share with others. As a result of developing our individuality, we have something unique to offer or add to the collectivity of humanity and the universe.

The beginning of the seasonal cycle occurs when the day becomes longer than the night at the Spring Equinox (Aries). At the Summer Solstice (Cancer), the day is at its longest; individuality has reached its height of personal focus and clarity. Then the night begins gradually to develop in length, symbolizing the individual's gradual social development. At the Fall Equinox (Libra), the night becomes longer than the day; this is where the individual begins to join socially with others to become something more than self. During the Winter Solstice (Capricorn), the day is at its shortest; the individual has fully integrated into the collective community. Through the winter the day begins to grow again in preparation for the rebirth of the individual impulse in the Spring.

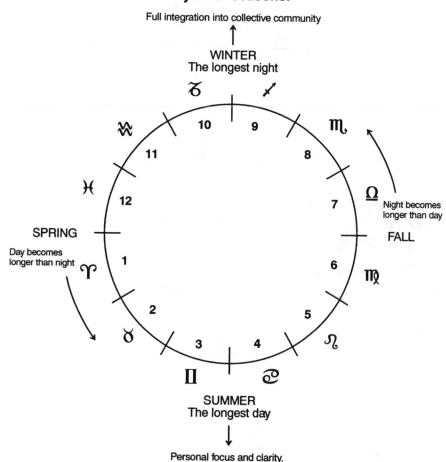

Cycle of Seasons:

Full integration into collective community

WINTER
The longest night

SPRING
Day becomes
longer than night

FALL

Night becomes
longer than day

SUMMER
The longest day

Personal focus and clarity.

figure 11

The signs derive their meanings not from the constellations of stars they are named after, but from the developmental phases of human growth symbolized by the cycle of the seasons.

The cycle of the seasons is more commonly referred to as the Tropical Zodiac. See Appendix II for a further explanation of the Tropical Zodiac.

This seasonal cycle with its interplay of day and night symbolizes human development in terms of psychological tendencies to act or behave in certain ways.

Section 4...The Developmental Potentials of the Signs

The Spring Signs

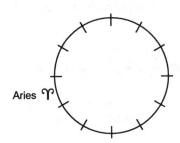

ARIES

The beginning thrust of a new cycle of personal developmental. Energy is spontaneously projected into a new direction.

Developmental Potentials:
Development of the ability to act with forcefulness, initiative and optimism. Self-assertion. Self-awareness.

Psychological Tendencies:
Assertive, energetic, initiating, optimistic, reckless, overbearing, aggressive, naive.

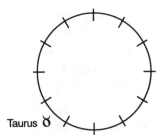

TAURUS

Energy is consolidated into form; the new personalized energy direction is established in the physical realm.

Developmental Potentials:

Development of the ability to relate to the physical world and to obtain resources to meet physical survival needs. The ability to be self-reliant.

Psychological Tendencies:

Resourceful, productive, sensual, stubborn, placid, self-indulgent, too materialistic.

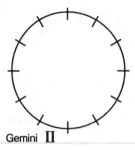

Gemini II

GEMINI

The energy form establishes connections within its immediate environment and develops the ability to co-ordinate its activities.

Developmental Potentials:

Development of the nervous system and rational mind to mentally perceive the immediate environment. The ability to learn, synthesize and communicate information. The developmental of mental and physical co-ordination.

Psychological Tendencies:

Intellectual, verbal, convincing, coordinated, superficial, nervous, scattered, fidgety.

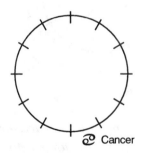

♋ Cancer

The Summer Signs

CANCER

A new sense of purpose and wholeness is established as a result of connections made in the previous phase. This new purpose builds toward fulfillment and culmination in later phases of the cycle.

Developmental Potentials:
Development of emotional wholeness and the ability to emotionally nurture and protect self. Individual clarity, motivation and a personal base of operation.

Psychological Tendencies:
Emotionally nurturing, social, personal, sensitive, insecure, defensive, shy, clinging.

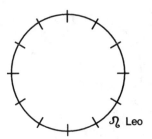

LEO

Energy is radiantly externalized as a result of its new purpose being more focused and whole.

Developmental Potentials:
Development of the ability to externalize emotions and express oneself in a warm, confident and creative manner.

Psychological Tendencies:
Extroverted, dramatic, playful, flamboyant, egotistical, conceited, demanding, childish.

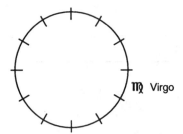

VIRGO

The flow and expression of energy are perfected through a process of improvement and refinement in preparation for meeting outside forces and other energy forms.

Developmental Potentials:
Development of the analytical faculties of the mind to solve physical problems and improve self-expression. The ability to be helpful and useful to others.

Psychological Tendencies:
Skillful, analytical, systematic, efficient, precise, self-condemning, too critical, too analytical, finicky.

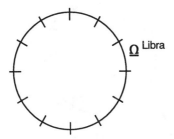

LIBRA

The meeting of opposites and other forms of energy occurs, requiring a process of interactive balancing and harmonizing.

Developmental Potentials:
Development of the ability to relate to others on an equal basis and to see another's needs as important as one's own needs. Development of harmony and balance within and with others.

Psychological Tendencies:
Social, agreeable, aesthetic, fair, indecisive, too compromising, manipulative, superficial.

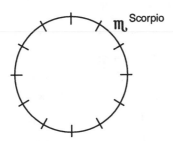

SCORPIO

Creative energy is released through the union of opposites, or two different energy forms. This union results in a transformation where the two single energy forms become more than what they are separately.

Developmental Potentials:
Development of the ability to merge self and resources with others, allowing for interdependence and sharing. Ability to become more through such a union than the self can be alone. Psychological transformations and the elevation of overly selfish desires through process of intimate interactions and unions.

Psychological Tendencies:
Emotionally intense, magnetic, intimate, psychological, secretive, sarcastic, revengeful, obsessive.

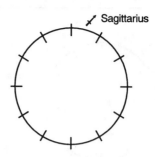

SAGITTARIUS

The energy form expands into larger realms as a result of the creative union of two separate forms.

Developmental Potentials:

Development of the ability to seek opportunities to expand in social-community realms. Development of the ability to use the abstract mind to establish goals and beliefs to live by.

Psychological Tendencies:

Philosophical, comprehensive, adventurous, religious, excessive, extravagant, irresponsible, insensitive.

The Winter Signs

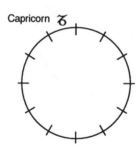

CAPRICORN

Energy reaches limits and boundaries in its creative expansion. Achieves fulfillment and culmination of purpose established in earlier phases.

Developmental Potentials:

Development of the ability to meet responsibilities to the community. Development of a reputation in the community through the achievement of personal goals.

Psychological Tendencies:

Ambitious, structured, realistic, organized, self-doubting, inhibited, guilty, too conservative.

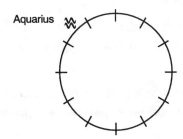

Aquarius

AQUARIUS

Rigid structures are changed or left behind as energy is oriented more toward the future.

Developmental Potentials:

Development of mental creativity and inventiveness through becoming open to the future. The ability to work with community goals and structures to make necessary changes for meeting the needs of all individuals.

Psychological Tendencies:

Progressive, humanistic, experimental, multi-cultural, impersonal, erratic, antisocial, detached.

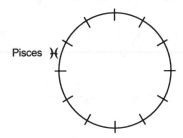

Pisces

PISCES

During a process of refinement where many of the old forms of expression are dissolved, energy develops into new levels beyond the here and now of the present cycle. This dissolution ultimately initiates a new cycle of energy development which builds on (what has been) certain forms that were developed in the previous cycle.

Developmental Potentials:

Development of the ability to be emotionally open and receptive to transcendental realms of the universe and the unconscious. Development of spiritual and psychic abilities.

Psychological Tendencies:

Emotional and spiritual refinement, empathetic, imaginative, compassionate, confused, moody, sacrificial, indiscriminate.

This is what you have explored:

1. Signs represent the innate tendency for you to act or behave in certain ways in order to develop particular psychological qualities and skills in your individuality.

2. Thinking of the signs as developmental potentials will help you understand where different sides of your psyche are in evolution toward full individuality.

3. You can more easily understand how any particular sign relates to the other signs depending upon which developmental phase of the sign. Aries is the 1st phase of a cycle and represents energy expressed in a spontaneous, assertive manner to allow an individual to take care of him or herself. Libra is the 7th phase, directly opposite the 1st phase, and represents the development of the ability to balance self-needs with the needs of others. Capricorn is the 10th phase and represents the potential of the individual to develop self-discipline and the ability to channel his or her assertiveness into responsible career structures that will benefit the larger, transpersonal community.

Section 5...The Cycle of the Day

The cycle of the day begins at sunrise. Twelve hours of daylight, sunset, and 12 night hours comprise the 24-hour cycle we commonly refer to as day.

In astrology this cycle of the day is also used as a vehicle to symbolize the focuses of activity an individual can choose to experience in order to more fully develop different sides of self.

We speak of the sun as rising in the east and setting in the west (visually a clockwise movement). The sun is not rising, of course. Rather, the earth is rotating counterclockwise, causing the sun to appear to rise through the sky.

Western astrology gives a counterclockwise order (movement) to the birth chart. If persons in the northern hemisphere face south toward the equator, the sun appears to rise on their left (east) and reach its highest point overhead at noon (south). It appears to set on the right (west) and reach its lowest point in the cycle at midnight (north).

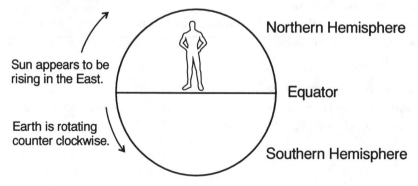

Sun appears to be rising in the East.

Earth is rotating counter clockwise.

Northern Hemisphere

Equator

Southern Hemisphere

figure 12

The Ascendant is the sunrise point, and directly opposite, the **Descendant** is the sunset point. The highest point overhead that the sun can reach in the daily cycle is called the **Midheaven**. Directly opposite is the midnight point, or **Nadir.**

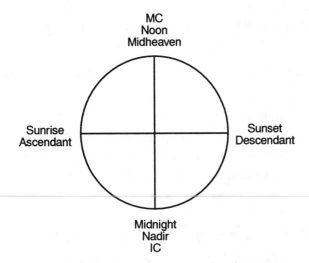

figure 14

Just as the cycle of the seasons is divided into twelve phases, called SIGNS, representing twelve developmental **ways of acting**, the cycle of the day is divided into twelve phases, called **HOUSES**, representing twelve developmental **focuses of activity**.

The twelve houses are divided going counterclockwise, the direction of the earth's rotation on its axis:

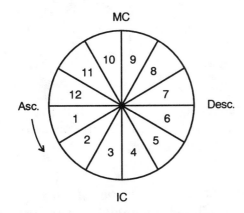

figure 15

A **focus of activity** refers to **WHERE** in a life a person focuses his or her energies or actions. A focus of activity refers to different types of outer experiences or environments in life. An individual may focus his or her energies in an activity in the home, in a political activity, in a recreational activity, in a business activity, in social activity that requires interaction with other people, or in activity that involves improving the physical body at an exercise gym. These different focuses of activity allow a person to develop more fully different sides of the self.

For Example:

Home activity might allow you to develop your inner sense of security and/or your ability to nurture children and other loved ones.

Political activity might allow you to develop your ability to contribute to the welfare of everyone in the community; the ability to see larger social realities and potentials as well as immediate self-oriented needs.

Recreational activity might allow you to develop the ability to relax, to enjoy life more fully.

While the houses indicate WHERE individuals tend to focus their energies or actions, the signs indicate **HOW** people tend to act. For example, you might focus on recreational activity in a social way, in a playful way, in a highly competitive way, in an active way, or in a sensual way.

Section 6...Developmental Potentials of the Houses

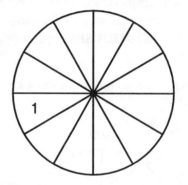

1st House

Developmental Potentials:
Developing personal assertion, drive and an approach to life that will eventually enable one to establish self-identity.

Focus of Activity:
The 1st house can refer to activities involving our personas, or personality projections (not necessarily what's inside), personal desires, self-centered interests, initiatives and spontaneous actions, and experiences of self-discovery.

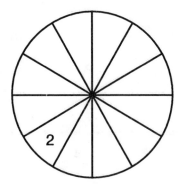

2nd House

Developmental Potentials:

The activities in life that allow an individual to develop self-reliance; the ability to establish self and survive in the physical realm.

Focus of Activity:

The 2nd house can refer to activities involving personal resources, money, physical body, sensuality, earning and spending habits, and the talent we rely on to make a living.

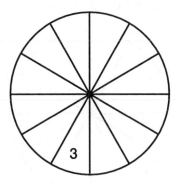

3rd House

Developmental Potentials:

Development of the nervous system, a rational and synthesizing mind, and the ability to coordinate self in the immediate environment.

Focus of Activity:

The 3rd house refers to activities involving personal communications, thinking and writing habits, forming connections and designs in the immediate environment, and activities in which we use a mental skill of coordination.

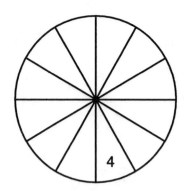

4th House

Developmental Potentials:
Development of a sense of emotional wholeness, individual focus and clarity, a personal base of operation, and an ability to protect and nurture self.

Focus of Activity:
The 4th house refers to activities involving the private self, personal needs and motivations, emotional security, home, family, how a person nurtures positive feelings about self, experiences in early childhood, or background which might have created a positive or negative self-image.

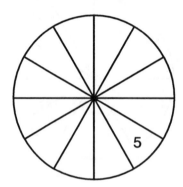

5th House

Developmental Potentials:
Activities in life that allow an individual to develop the ability to express and externalize inner, personal emotions in a unique, individual, confident manner.

Focus of Activity:
The 5th house refers to activities involving creative flow and self-expression, pleasures, personal displays, game playing, giving and getting attention in love, and ways to relax.

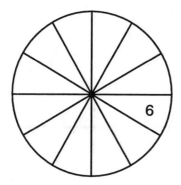

6th House

Developmental Potentials:
Improving and perfecting personal creative expression, and analytical, mental faculties for solving everyday life problems.

Focus of Activity:
The 6th house refers to self-improvement, routines, work situations, the kinds of therapies one may use for preventive and healing health care, the kinds of experiences that may cause physical sickness, how one overcomes this sickness, and adjusts to personal crises.

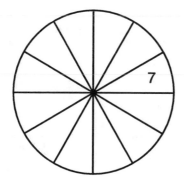

7th House

Developmental Potentials:
Development of social awareness and ability to consider and understand others' interests and needs.

Focus of Activity:
The 7th house refers to activities involving one-to-one encounters, how to relate to others, cooperation, competitiveness, finding a mate and seeking completion in others.

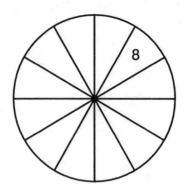

8th House

Developmental Potentials:
Developing the ability to become more than self through union with others and intense psychological transformations.

Focus of Activity:
The 8th house refers to activities involving shared emotional and physical resources, emotional releases, psychological transformations or repressions, sexuality, rituals leading to peak experiences — often by linking emotional states with others.

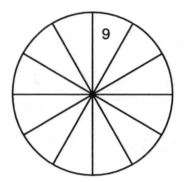

9th House

Developmental Potentials:
Expansion of self in search of social opportunity, meaning, truth and ideals.

Focus of Activity:
The 9th house refers to activities involving the abstract mind, developing a belief system, long-distance travels (physically or mentally), publishing, higher education, laws, and how we seek opportunities to grow and expand.

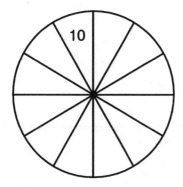

10th House

Developmental Potentials:
Develops the ability to give opportunities, ideals, and personal motivations concrete form in the eyes of others.

Focus of Activity:
The 10th house refers to activities involving career achievements, community position, reputation, relationships with authority figures, and how we handle community responsibility.

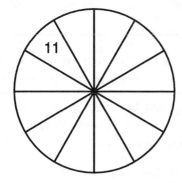

11th House

Developmental Potentials:
The ability to orient community efforts and achievements to benefit all of humanity, and to be open to new possibilities and changes of the future.

Focus of Activity:
The 11th house refers to activities involving humanitarian ideals and social causes, experimentation, inventiveness, how to relate to future possibilities and sudden changes, creativity, mental flashes, insight.

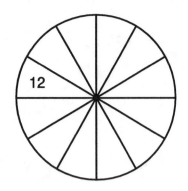

12th House

Developmental Potentials:
Awareness of and use of universal talents; freedom from the past by facing the unknowns of universal realms; the collective unconscious and the future.

Focus of Activity:
The 12th house refers to activities involving inner visions, dreams, universal imagination, spiritual and psychic experiences, and "magical" talents; aloneness and solitude as we free ourselves from community restraints and barriers as well as from psychological restrictions and repressions.

This is what you have explored:

1. Houses represent activities or areas of life that will develop particular psychological qualities and skills in your individuality.

2. The cycle of the day can be divided into two phases of development (hemispheres), four phases of development (quadrants) and twelve phases of development (houses).

3. You can understand the meaning of each house by knowing its developmental phase in the whole cycle of the day.

Section 7...Cycles Of Planets

In astrology planets symbolize the **psychological functions** of an individual's psyche, such as an individual's ability to receive and absorb as well as to act.

Note: With the evolution of society has come the recognition that all disabled individuals possess these psychological functions although the physical and mental condition of the individual may interfere with their full expression.

From the earth's perspective we see the Sun and the Moon, and therefore we include them as two of the 10 planets that are analyzed in the birth chart. The following is a list of these planets and their psychological functions.

PLANETS	PSYCHOLOGICAL FUNCTIONS
The **SUN** ☉ symbolizes the individual's	**capacity to be unique; to become an individual.**
The **MOON** ☽ symbolizes the individual's	**capacity for emotional expression.**
MERCURY ☿ symbolizes the individual's	**capacities to think and communicate rationally.**
VENUS ♀ symbolizes the individual's	**capacities for sensual and social receptivity.**
MARS ♂ symbolizes the individual's	**capacity to be assertive.**
JUPITER ♃ symbolizes the individual's	**capacities for expansion and abstract thinking.**
SATURN ♄ symbolizes the individual's	**capacities for self-discipline and handling difficult life tests with endurance.**
URANUS ♅ symbolizes the individual's	**capacity to mentally perceive creative potentials for the future**
NEPTUNE ♆ symbolizes the individual's	**capacity to be receptive to dreams, visions, and inspirations.**
PLUTO ♀ symbolizes the individual's	**capacity for major psychological transformations.**

Most of the planets (Moon to Saturn) complete more than one orbit or cycle during an individual's life. The 84-year cycle of Uranus can be completed during an individual's lifetime but Neptune and Pluto will only complete portions of their cycles.

Viewed from the earth, as we move from shorter to longer cycles of the planets, the increasing length of each planet's cycle symbolizes psychological functions that allow an individual to relate to ever-widening and complex spheres of life: personal, social, community, spiritual.

Let's explore the meaning of the planets in terms of the increasing length of their cycles as viewed from the earth:

☽ MOON – 29 Days

The receptive psyche of the newborn baby. The fastest cycle symbolizes the repeating process of life, the development of habit patterns and psychological conditioning as a result of early environmental influences, and subconscious memories. The Moon is the closest "planet" to earth and is said to symbolize the formation of the emotional nature with its many moods and changes, acting as a lens through which one distributes and expresses the energy of other parts of the psyche in daily life.

The Moon should eventually reflect the essence of selfhood, symbolized by the Sun, through the development of individuality (rather than merely symbolizing conditioned responses to the daily environment).

Psychological Function: Emotional expression and responsiveness.

☿ MERCURY – 88 Days

Development of the nervous system, a sense of coordination, allowing the newborn baby to make first extensions, movements and sounds in the environment.

Eventually this psychological function allows one to think rationally and analytically; and further, to make use of abstract and intuitive knowledge, to communicate feelings, imagination and visions.

Psychological Function: Rational thinking and communication.

♀ VENUS – 225 Days

Relating to and evaluating what is outside self through physical senses, feeling attractions, repulsions, comfort, discomfort, pleasure and pain. The newborn baby begins to develop likes and dislikes, especially in diet, and what s/he sees, hears, touches. As we mature, this psychological function allows us to relate to others' needs and to develop a sense of beauty and aesthetics.

Psychological Function: Social receptivity and sense of relatedness.

☉ SUN – 365 Days

The Sun symbolizes the essence of the individual; vitality has been established. As this essence is developed, the "light" and power continue to increase, serving as an integrating force for all the other psychological functions. By the time the Sun completes its first cycle after birth, the young child is perhaps taking his or her first steps alone; an expression of this vital and integrative psychological function.

Psychological Function: Capacity to develop individual essence and purpose.

♂ MARS – 687 Days

Physical development of the child's assertiveness and ability to use energy for purposeful action to get what s/he desires. Could correspond to the "terrible twos." This Mars psychological function eventually allows sexual expression and release. The Pluto transforming side of nature will be continually working on the Mars side of self to elevate its willpower so that it can be joined in a positive union with others.

Psychological Function: To act assertively and forcefully on one's own behalf; to express personal drives.

♃ JUPITER – 11.86 Years

The ability to expand into social, and eventually, abstract realms to assimilate, understand and learn from new experiences. With completion of Jupiter's first cycle, around the age of 12, the growing child expands from the family in search of new social opportunities, initiating the teenage years of social exploration. With the completion of **Jupiter's second cycle** at the age of 24, further expansions are made in search of an understanding of our individuality and opportunities to establish ourselves in the community. Jupiter's return through life symbolizes the potential for new levels of understanding.

Psychological Function: Self growth and expression. Abstract mind.

♄ SATURN – 29.46 Years

The ability to limit, discipline and control expansion. Development of sense of timing, maturity, and ego structures. Three cycles of Saturn symbolize three levels of maturity that the individual can achieve. **First Saturn Cycle** (Birth to 28 years): Individual Maturing. The realization of limits. An individual must free him or herself from expectations and conditioning that are not in tune with his or her essence and purpose. This allows development of a unique ego structure. **Second Saturn Cycle** (28 years to 56 years): Social Maturing. After having been freed from the collective conditioning of the past during the first 28 years of life, the next 28 years mark a gradual return to the social collective, but on the individual's own terms. Social achievement of personal goals can be established. **Third Saturn Cycle** (56 years to 84 years): Spiritual Maturing. Measures the gradual return to the universal collective. The detachment from concrete achievements socially, gradually developing maturity and wisdom on a transcendental level.

Psychological Function: Self-discipline and sense of responsibility.

The psychological functions listed above allow the individual to take care of him or her self, to develop relationships, achieve expansion and success, take advantage of opportunities and meet responsibilities to society. The following psychological functions, symbolized by the three outer planets, Uranus, Neptune, and Pluto, allow the individual to achieve universal awareness by transcending the limitations of selfishness and rigid emotional and social patterns. For many individuals these psychological functions are experienced as unconscious urges verses conscious choices of the psyche.

♅ *URANUS – 84 years*

Unconscious urge to break free from rigid structures to allow a continual process of individuation. Can be experienced as disruptive, erratic, impulses. The universal mind allows for futuristic, progressive, inventive thinking.

Psychological Function: Higher mind. Universal mental perception.

♆ *NEPTUNE – 164.8 Years*

Unconscious urge to emotionally experience universal awareness to dissolve the limits of the ego. The function of the psyche that is receptive to the universality of dreams, visions, psychic and spiritual realms. Usually experienced as moodiness, confusion, hypersensitivity, unreality. Yet Neptune can give a personality "magical" imaginative qualities when operating positively, and a refined universal sense of beauty, empathy and compassion.

Psychological Function: Higher emotional nature. Universal emotional receptivity.

♇ *PLUTO – 248 Years*

Unconscious urge to eliminate lower emotions by facing and transforming the dark side of self. Metamorphosis of selfishness in line with universal purposes, creating universal power in the individual. Can be experienced as obsessions, and urges for complete dominance and power over others. When operating positively, it seeks union with others and the universe, the losing of ego in peak experiences. Just as the Sun is considered to point to the individual purpose, Pluto points to the universal purpose.

Psychological Function: Capacity for psychological transformation.

Meaningful Groups

One way to understand the psychological functions is to look at them in meaningful groups.

Group 1: ☉ ☽ ☿ ♀ ♂

Represent personal and interpersonal psychological functions. People most noticeably operate with these functions.

Group 2: ♃ ♄

Represent societal psychological functions. As people mature, they begin to operate more positively and securely with these aspects of themselves.

Group 3: ♅ ♆ ♀

Represents transcendental/universal psychological functions. These are usually the unconscious sides of self, which require further maturity to allow them to develop and to be used positively.

---

1. ☉ essence of self
   ☽ reflection of this essence of individuality in everyday life

2. ☽ capacity to nurture self with positive feelings; child within
   ♄ capacity to perfect and discipline self with realistic demands; parent within

3. ♀ appreciation, love
   ♂ personal desires; sexuality

4. ☿ rational, concrete mind
   ♃ abstract, philosophical mind

5. ♃ social expansion
   ♄ social limits and responsibility

6. ♄ consolidation and resistance to change
   ♅ progressiveness and openness to change

7. ♀ sense of safety and security
   ♀ the urge to take the risk of emotional transformation through uniting with others for a collective purpose

8. ☉ subjective sense of individuality; urge for self- expression
   ♅ objective sense of planetary and universal consciousness; urge for group creativity

9. ☿ mental analysis; sense of surface realities
   ♆ universal imagination and psychic awareness; sense of intangible realities

10. ♀ personal love and aesthetics
    ♆ transcendental, universal love and aesthetics

11. ♂ personal willpower and sexual drive
    ♀ universal willpower, urge for sexual union

Meaningful Pairs

The parts of the psyche (symbolized by Jupiter, Saturn, Uranus, Neptune and Pluto), that allow us to operate in social, impersonal, or transpersonal realms, can present problems during childhood for any of us who have these community/transpersonal functions emphasized in our charts. The undeveloped ego of the child could experience pressures so difficult to handle that in order to survive it creates defense mechanisms to handle the stresses, or it succumbs to the pressures.

The young child's ego is not developed enough to consciously control and handle the functions which require maturity and individual centeredness. Thus, these impersonal and transpersonal functions interfere with the appropriate self-centeredness of the young ego. Negative psychological patterns caused by these pressures can continue into adulthood until one consciously faces them and seeks to transform them into more positive psychological traits.

Each of the community/transpersonal functions may have the following negative effects on the undeveloped ego:

Jupiter — tendency toward excessiveness.

Saturn — tendency toward self-doubt, guilt, and a feeling of being controlled by one's environment.

Uranus — tendency toward unpredictability, erratic, rebellious, unusual behavior.

Neptune — tendency toward over-passivity, surrendering the ego to unconscious diffusion, hyper-sensitivity, extreme impressionability.

Pluto — tendency toward power struggles, revengeful feelings, and the release of pent-up emotions in explosive outbursts.

Since Pluto represents such a complex function within the psyche, I will describe further some of the ways it operates.

Pluto represents the psychological function that urges and allows the psyche to experience psychological transformations:

The process of psychological transformation involves:

  • a change from something old to something new.

The old patterns and habits have to be let go, eliminated in order to make way for the new to develop. Therefore, the Pluto functions challenge us to discard old psychological patterns, repressed emotions, painful childhood memories and resulting defensive blocks in order to allow for new, more positive psychological patterns to develop.

  • rechanneling overly selfish desires into the capacity to bond emotionally with another person in a loving manner.

Each individual needs to be self-oriented and assertive at times in order to satisfy basic survival needs and to be able to develop his/her individuality. However, an individual must be able to elevate, direct and transform these selfish drives into receptive emotional love. Such emotional receptivity is powerful and passionate in nature because it involves the joining of opposites both within the psyche and with another person. Such a merging results in a special release of emotional energy that can be both creative and regenerating.

- bringing to surface the "darker" sides of the psyche; the sides that we must face, accept, elevate and integrate within the conscious self.

Each human being is capable of acting in negative overly selfish, extreme, repressed, even hurtful or violent ways. However each of us also has urges within our psyches to act in more balanced and positive ways, to have love and compassion for others, and to have a sense of limits and responsibility. But it is the Pluto function that allows the psyche to emotionally contain overly selfish desires and drives, and to elevate these negative tendencies into more positive expressions.

If the Plutonian process of facing and transforming the dark sides of self becomes blocked or hindered it can lead to repressed emotions which in turn can lead to a tendency to explode when pent-up emotions reach a peak. It can also lead to power struggles within the psyche, which are often projected onto others.

- merging and blending opposites within the psyche

One opposition within the psyche is between the conscious and unconscious side of self. Another is between the self-centered and the loving, receptive side of self, the receptive side being capable of deep emotional creative unions with other individual.

The process of merging and blending the opposites causes a transformation, a change from something old to something new. This function allows us to release energy on a more creative, purposeful level as a result of the union of opposites within the psyche.

- the capacity to develop mutually transforming relationships with others.

The Pluto function urges one to develop intimate, emotional unions with others. These unions allow the psyche to experience how it is to feel whole and balanced. As was noted above, close, intimate relationships challenge both individuals to transform selfish drives. Psychological and emotional bonding with others also helps us to develop sides that we are not naturally inclined to develop. While the psyche has a tendency to project onto others the sides of self that a person is lacking, Pluto is the function that challenges the psyche to develop what is lacking within. As we become more balanced and self-actualized, whole; we are able to bring more to the relationship.

In your birth chart the sign of Pluto tells you a **way of being or acting** by which you may experience major psychological transformation and changes during your life. The house position of Pluto tells you a **focus of activity** in which you may experience major transformations.

This is what you have explored:

1. Planets (including the Sun and the Moon) represent psychological functions of your psyche.

2. Your psychological functions can be understood by the relationship that the cycles of the planets have to each other as viewed from earth.

3. The planets with the shortest cycles represent psychological functions that allow an individual to attend to personal needs. The progression of the planets with increasing length of their cycles symbolize the individual's capacity to function in ever-enlarging realms of life (social, community, universal).

Section 8...
Planets In Signs And Houses

The **PLANETS** *represent ten* **psychological functions (capacities to act).**

The **SIGNS** *represent twelve developmental* **ways of acting.**

The **HOUSES** *represent twelve developmental* **focuses of activity.**

The planets symbolize the functions of the psyche that allow an individual to act in certain ways (planet's sign position) and to be focused on certain types of activities (planets' house position).

For example, Mars represents a capacity for the individual to be assertive. **How** a person is assertive depends on its sign position. **Where** a person focuses his or her assertiveness depends on its house position.

If Mars is in Gemini, the individual will have a tendency to express his or her assertiveness mentally and communicatively. He or she may be a forceful speaker and writer, and perhaps may be verbally argumentative.

If Mars is in Scorpio, the individual may have a tendency to keep his or her assertiveness emotionally controlled until it can be expressed in an emotionally powerful manner. Sometimes Mars in Scorpio suggests that anger and assertiveness might be kept too emotionally controlled until it overflows in a volcanic, explosive expression.

If Mars is in the 5th house, the individual might focus his or her assertiveness on recreational, playful activities, such as sports or other types of active games.

If Mars is in the 10th house, the individual might focus his or her assertiveness on achieving success in career activities. This assertiveness might be channeled into activities requiring self-discipline and responsibility.

In your birth chart each planet has **both** a SIGN and a HOUSE POSITION. Therefore, each of your psychological functions has natural tendencies to act in certain ways and to focus on certain activities.

- If Mars is in Gemini in the fifth house, the individual will have a tendency to focus his or her assertiveness on playful and creative activities in a mental and communicative way. Word games or getting into playful discussions and debates with friends would be enjoyable choices. The individual might like to read and/or write satire or other writings that are forceful and hard-hitting.

- If Mars is in Gemini in the tenth house, the individual will have a tendency to express assertiveness by focusing on career activities and achievements in a mental and communicative way. His or her career might involve an ability to be forceful and direct with the spoken or written word, such as in courtroom situations, in directing or managing others, or in news reporting.

Using the exercises that come later in this book you will be able to determine your planets' signs and house positions and analyze the meanings these positions have for you.

Section 9...Rulership

Each planet corresponds in meaning to a particular sign and house. Mars is the psychological function most similar to the first phase of development. Therefore it is referred to as "ruling" Aries and the 1st house. Each planet is said to "rule" a particular sign and house (some planets rule 2 houses).

	SIGNS		RULING PLANET	RELATED HOUSE
A	Aries	♂	Mars	1st
B	Taurus	♀	Venus	2nd
C	Gemini	☿	Mercury	3rd
D	Cancer	☽	Moon	4th
E	Leo	☉	Sun	5th
F	Virgo	☿	Mercury	6th
G	Libra	♀	Venus	7th
H	Scorpio	♀	Pluto	8th
I	Sagittarius	♃	Jupiter	9th
J	Capricorn	♄	Saturn	10th
K	Aquarius	♅	Uranus	11th
L	Pisces	♆	Neptune	12th

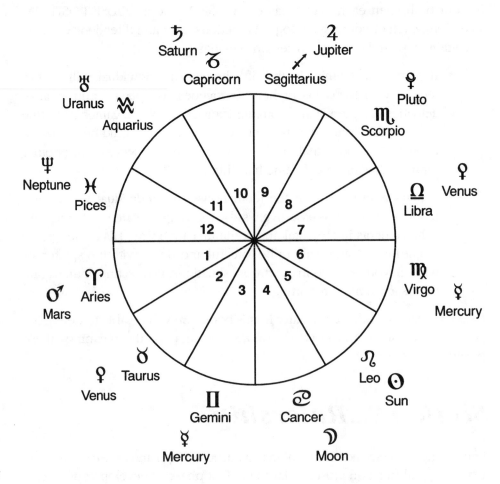

Fig 16

In the birth chart each planet is located in a sign and house position. These positions will not necessarily be in the sign and house that a planet rules. See Appendix II How to Read a Birth Chart Form for further explanations regarding the signs and house positions of planets.

When a planet is found in a sign or house that it "rules," there is potential strength or ease of expression attributed to the psychological function represented. For example: If Mars is in Aries in your birth chart, the psychological function Mars (which represents self-assertion) will be strengthened by the Aries developmental inclination to act forcefully.

A planet may be in a sign or house that it does not rule, but that is compatible with its nature. Therefore the psychological function represented by the planet could have an easier time being expressed in a positive and creative way. For example: If Mars is in Gemini in your birth chart the assertive energy of Mars is compatible with Gemini's developmental inclination to gather and connect ideas in a dynamic intellectual manner.

If a planet is in a sign or house that is discordant to its nature, conscious adjustments have to be made to blend the two different qualities into a positive expression. For example: If Mars is found in Pisces in your birth chart, the passive psychological energy qualities of Pisces would be discordant with the assertive capacity that Mars represents; yet a positive expression could result when the Mars psychological function is blended with the Piscian psychological qualities. Mars energy could activate Pisces' receptivity to universal vision and images; or conscious blending could occur between self-needs with the needs to selflessly serve others. Psychological emotional complexes created by tensions between the two psychological qualities may first have to be overcome.

Section 10...
The Law of Correspondences
(As Above, So Below)

Many people who are unfamiliar with the deeper dimensions of astrology are often concerned about how the planets can tell anything about a person. How do the cycles of the solar system mirror the psychological nature and potentials of an individual?

The **Law of Correspondences**, formulated in metaphysical disciplines since ancient times, means that the quality of the larger whole or cycle is reflected within its lesser wholes or cycles. One does not actually cause something to happen in the other — it's all one and the same.

Imagine that in a small town there is a huge clock in a tower that is showing 6:00 a.m. In homes and buildings all over the town smaller clocks and watches should be showing the same time. But the tower clock is not **causing** the smaller clocks and watches to show 6:00 a.m.; rather each watch and clock is reflecting the same quality or moment of time from its own position.

The individual psyche is like a solar system in itself: a whole consisting of parts, such as the rational mind (Mercury), or the emotions (Moon), each in different phases of development. In turn, the whole of the individual psyche exists within a larger whole of the actual solar system with its own complex relationships of cycles (See Figure 17).

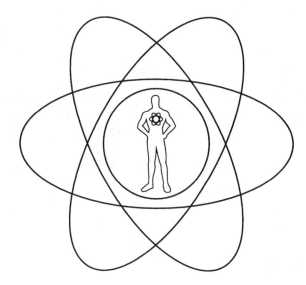

Fig 17

Just as in the example of the clocks, the planetary cycles of our solar system do not cause you to be a certain way; rather the potentials of your individuality are reflected in the quality of time at your moment of birth (and location). Your birth chart captures the **quality of time** of our solar system at your moment of birth where you were born.

The quality of time is symbolized in your birth chart by the interrelation of the major cycles of our solar system. Quality of time assumes meaning from the phases reflected in the major cycles of our solar system at any given moment.

In Chapters Four and Six of this book you will be able to use exercises to identify the developmental potentials of your psyche as symbolized by the signs and house positions of your planets. You will then be able to translate these **developmental potentials** into your **natural inclinations** to act in certain ways (sign positions) and within certain focuses of activity (house positions).

Initial Steps In Interpreting Your Birth Chart: Holistic Overview — Your Natural Inclinations

If you have been around people who know astrology you've probably heard them say, "Oh, that's just like your Moon in Virgo: detecting every flaw in someone's personality within the first five minutes of meeting them." Or "Your Pisces is so ethereal. I just wish I new what reality you are tuned to most of the time." Or, "You'd better try controlling your Venus in Leo at this party. Remember you're with me. You haven't been hired to entertain the guests."

Astrological symbols and terminology can seem like meaningless language to a beginner. Before you can interpret the key symbolism of your birth chart you must be able to translate the astrological symbols into everyday language. Once you have translated them, you will more easily be able to explore the meanings and potentials these symbols have for you.

The exercises in this section are meant to give you an overview of the different sides of your psyche.

You will be able to see how each of your psychological functions (PLANETS) is:

- inclined to act or behave (SIGN POSITIONS)
      and are

- inclined to focus on a particular type of activity in life (HOUSE POSITIONS)

Remember, this is the first step of interpretation. Once you finish, you will most likely have questions regarding the symbolism and the interpretations. You will find some of these questions answered as you use this book and the other volumes of this series. As mentioned in the preface of this book, allow yourself time to integrate and use this new model.

In the next chapter I have addressed some common questions that beginning students have when they begin to work the astrological symbolism of their birth chart. These questions will mean more to you after you have used these two exercises to begin interpreting your birth chart.

The Sign Of Your Planets — Your Inclinations To Act In Certain Ways

EXERCISE 1:

On pages 62 and 63 are ten sentences, one for each planet. Complete these sentences with keywords describing the way of acting that seems most appropriate for the sign in which each planet is located:

Step 1: Write the symbol for your Sun's sign in the appropriate blank space.

Step 2: In the margins of these two pages are keywords for each of the signs. Choose one or more of the keywords under the sign in which your natal Sun is located and write the word(s) in the blanks to complete the sentence associated with the Sun.

Step 3: Continue this process with the rest of the planets.

The House Positions Of Your Planets — Your Inclinations To Focus On Certain Activities in Life

EXERCISE 2:

On pages 66 and 67 are ten sentences, one for each planet. Complete these sentences with keywords describing the life activities or experiences of the house in which the planet is located:

Step 1: Determine the house position of the Sun in your birth chart and write the house number (1-12) in the appropriate blank space.

Step 2: In the margins of these two pages are keywords for each of the signs. Choose one or more of the keywords under the sign in which your natal Sun is located and write the word(s) in the blanks to complete the sentence associated with the Sun.

Step 3: Continue this process with the rest of the planets.

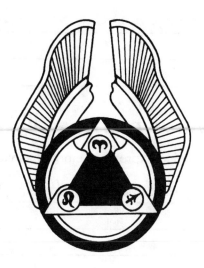

This page is intentionally blank.

PLANETS - SIGN POSITION - (Alice's Birth Chart Example)

ARIES
Assertively
With Initiative
Energetically
Optimistically
Overbearingly
Impulsively

TAURUS
Self-Reliantly
Sensually
Resourcefully
Productively
Possessively
Stubbornly

GEMINI
Rationally
Persuasively
Verbally
Adaptably
Scattered
Shallowly

CANCER
Nurturingly
With Emotional Clarity
Responsively
Caringly
Insecurely
Defensively

LEO
Confidently
Dramatically
Self Expressively
Creatively
Egotistically
Domineeringly

VIRGO
Efficiently
Precisely
In a Serving Manner
Self-Improvingly
Too Critically
Perfectionistically

SUN SIGN POSITION ♊ *Gemini*

I am inclined to express my urge to become an individual by acting

persuasively, verbally, rationally.

_____

_____

MOON SIGN POSITION ♏ *Scorpio*

I am inclined to express my emotional nature by acting

intensely and magnetically.

_____

_____

MERCURY SIGN POSITION ♋ *Cancer*

I am inclined to use my logical, rational mind by acting

caringly, responsively (insecurely).

_____

_____

VENUS SIGN POSITION ♋ *Cancer*

I am inclined to express my social nature by acting

responsively and nurturingly (defensively).

_____

_____

MARS SIGN POSITION ♑ *Capricorn*

I am inclined to be assertive by acting

with organization, responsibly (with self-doubt).

_____

JUPITER SIGN POSITION ♋ Cancer

I am inclined to expand beyond my circumstances in life by acting

caringly and nurturingly.

_____

_____

SATURN SIGN POSITION ♏ Scorpio

I am inclined to be responsible and disciplined by acting

intensley and with emotional depth.

_____

_____

URANUS SIGN POSITION ♋ Cancer

I am inclined to use my higher, inventive mind by acting

with emotional clarity and caringly.

_____

_____

NEPTUNE SIGN POSITION ♎ Libra

I am inclined to express my higher, universal emotional nature by acting

aesthetically and harmonizingly.

_____

_____

PLUTO SIGN POSITION ♌ Leo

I am inclined to express my capacity for psychological transformation by acting

creatively and dramatically.

_____

_____

_____

LIBRA
Sociably
Cooperatively
Harmonizingly
Aesthetically
Superficially
Indecisively

SCORPIO
With Emotional Depth
Magnetically
Intensely
Interdependently
Obsessively
Repressively

SAGITTARIUS
Enthusiastically
Expansively
Knowledgeably
Adventurously
Excessively
Dogmatically

CAPRICORN
With Organization
Responsibly
Orderly
Constructively
With Self-Doubt
With Inhibition

AQUARIUS
Inventively
Socially-Concerned
Experimentally
Multi-Culturally
With Eccentricity
Erratically

PISCES
Imaginatively
Compassionately
Spiritually
With Confusion
Indiscriminately

PLANETS - SIGN POSITION

ARIES
Assertively
With Initiative
Energetically
Optimistically
Overbearingly
Impulsively

TAURUS
Self-Reliantly
Sensually
Resourcefully
Productively
Possessively
Stubbornly

GEMINI
Rationally
Persuasively
Verbally
Adaptably
Scattered
Shallowly

CANCER
Nurturingly
With Emotional Clarity
Responsively
caringly
Insecurely
Defensively

LEO
Confidently
Dramatically
Self Expressively
Creatively
Egotistically
Domineeringly

VIRGO
Efficiently
Precisely
In a Serving Manner
Self-Improvingly
Too Critically
Perfectionistically

SUN SIGN POSITION _____

I am inclined to express my urge to become an individual by acting

_____
_____
_____

MOON SIGN POSITION _____

 I am inclined to express my emotional nature by acting

_____
_____
_____

MERCURY SIGN POSITION _____

I am inclined to use my logical, rational mind by acting

_____
_____
_____

VENUS SIGN POSITION _____

I am inclined to express my social nature by acting

_____
_____
_____

MARS SIGN POSITION _____

I am inclined to be assertive by acting

_____
_____
_____

Astrology for the Absolute Beginner

JUPITER SIGN POSITION _____

I am inclined to expand beyond my circumstances in life by acting

_____

_____

_____

SATURN SIGN POSITION _____

I am inclined to be responsible and disciplined by acting

_____

_____

_____

URANUS SIGN POSITION _____

I am inclined to use my higher, inventive mind by acting

_____

_____

_____

NEPTUNE SIGN POSITION _____

I am inclined to express my higher, universal emotional nature by acting

_____

_____

_____

PLUTO SIGN POSITION _____

I am inclined to express my capacity for psychological transformation by acting

_____

_____

_____

_____

_____

LIBRA
Sociably
Cooperatively
Harmonizingly
Aesthetically
Superficially
Indecisively

SCORPIO
With Emotional Depth
Magnetically
Intensely
Interdependently
Obsessively
Repressively

SAGITTARIUS
Enthusiastically
Expansively
Knowledgeably
Adventurously
Excessively
Dogmatically

CAPRICORN
With Organization
Responsibly
Orderly
Constructively
With Self-Doubt
With Inhibition

AQUARIUS
Inventively
Socially-Concerned
Experimentally
Multi-Culturally
With eccentricity
Erratically

PISCES
imaginatively
Compassionately
Spiritually
With Confusion
Indiscriminately

1ST HOUSE
Self Discovery
Personal Freedom
Personality Projection
My Independence

2ND HOUSE
Financial Resources
Survival Needs
Sensuality
Self-Reliance

3RD HOUSE
Personal Communications
Thinking/Writing Habits
Rational Perception
Mental Coordination

4TH HOUSE
Personal Emotional Needs
Personal Nurturing
Emotional Security
Home and Family

5TH HOUSE
Self Expression
Self Confidence
Exchanging Special
Attention

6TH HOUSE
Self Improvement
Work Habits
Mental Analysis
Physical Healing

PLANETS - HOUSE POSITION — (Alice's Birth Chart Example)

SUN HOUSE POSITION _____ *11th house* _____

I am inclined to express my urge to become an individual by focusing on

mass communications and multi-cultural communications.

_____

_____

MOON HOUSE POSITION _____ *3rd house* _____

I am inclined to express my emotional nature by focusing on

personal communications, mental co-ordination.

_____

_____

MERCURY HOUSE POSITION _____ *11th house* _____

I am inclined to use my logical, rational mind by focusing on

mental inventiveness and mass communication.

_____

_____

VENUS HOUSE POSITION _____ *12th house* _____

I am inclined to express my social nature by focusing on

*visions, dreams, compassionate love and universal
imagination.*

_____

MARS HOUSE POSITION _____ *5th house* _____

I am inclined to be assertive by focusing on

personal creativity and self-expression.

_____

_____

JUPITER HOUSE POSITION _____11th house_____

I am inclined to expand beyond my circumstances in life by focusing on

multi-cultural connections and mass communication.

SATURN HOUSE POSITION _____3rd house_____

I am inclined to be responsible and disciplined by focusing on

thinking/writing habits, rational perceptions and self-education.

URANUS HOUSE POSITION _____12th house_____

I am inclined to use my higher, inventive mind by focusing on

spiritual realities and universal imagination.

NEPTUNE HOUSE POSITION _____3rd house_____

I am inclined to express my higher, universal emotional nature by focusing on

thinking and writing habits and personal communications.

PLUTO HOUSE POSITION _____1st house_____

I am inclined to express my capacity for psychological transformation by focusing on

self-discovery and personal freedoms.

7TH HOUSE
Social Relationship
One-to-One Encounters
Needs of Others
Cooperation

8TH HOUSE
Emotional Sharing
Physical/Emotional Union
Shared Resources
Interdependence

9TH HOUSE
Opportunities for Growth
Social Expansion
Abstract Mind
Seeking Understanding

10TH HOUSE
Career/Profession
Responsibility to Community
Social Limits
Authority

11TH HOUSE
Community's Responsibility To All Individuals
Mental Inventiveness
Multi-Cultural Connections
Mass Communications

12TH HOUSE
Spiritual Reality
Visions and Dreams
The Unconscious
Compassionate Love

PLANETS - HOUSE POSITION

1ST HOUSE
Self Discovery
Personal Freedom
Personality Projection
My Independence

2ND HOUSE
Financial Resources
Survival Needs
Sensuality
Self-Reliance

3RD HOUSE
Personal Communications
Thinking/Writing Habits
Rational Perception
Mental Coordination

4TH HOUSE
Personal Emotional Needs
Personal Nurturing
Emotional Security
Home and Family

5TH HOUSE
Self Expression
Self Confidence
Exchanging Special
Attention

6TH HOUSE
Self Improvement
Work Habits
Mental Analysis
Physical Healing

SUN HOUSE POSITION _____

I am inclined to express my urge to become an individual by focusing on

_____

_____

_____

MOON HOUSE POSITION _____

I am inclined to express my emotional nature by focusing on

_____

_____

_____

MERCURY HOUSE POSITION _____

I am inclined to use my logical, rational mind by focusing on

_____

_____

_____

VENUS HOUSE POSITION _____

I am inclined to express my social nature by focusing on

_____

_____

_____

MARS HOUSE POSITION _____

I am inclined to be assertive by focusing on

_____

_____

_____

JUPITER HOUSE POSITION _____

I am inclined to expand beyond my circumstances in life by focusing on

_____

_____

_____

SATURN HOUSE POSITION _____

I am inclined to be responsible and disciplined by focusing on

_____

_____

_____

URANUS HOUSE POSITION _____

I am inclined to use my higher, inventive mind by focusing on

_____

_____

_____

NEPTUNE HOUSE POSITION _____

I am inclined to express my higher, universal emotional nature by focusing on

_____

_____

_____

PLUTO HOUSE POSITION _____

I am inclined to express my capacity for psychological transformation by focusing on

_____

_____

_____

_____

_____

7TH HOUSE

Social Relationship

One-to-One Encounters

Needs of Others

Cooperation

8TH HOUSE

Emotional Sharing

Physical/Emotional Union

Shared Resources

Interdependence

9TH HOUSE

Opportunities for Growth

Social Expansion

Abstract Mind

Seeking Understanding

10TH HOUSE

Career/Profession

Responsibility to Community

Social Limits

Authority

11TH HOUSE

Community's Responsibility To All Individuals

Mental Inventiveness

Multi-Cultural Connections

Mass Communications

12TH HOUSE

Spiritual Reality

Visions and Dreams

The Unconscious

Compassionate Love

Common Questions And Guidelines For Interpretation

You have determined the signs and house positions of your planets and have begun to translate these symbols into everyday language. The following guidelines based upon commonly asked questions will assist you in interpreting the meaning of your birth chart.

Question 1: *How do I know which words to choose when I fill in the blanks?*

There are no right choices other than what is right for you at the moment.

You are not being asked to define yourself in a rigid and deterministic manner. You are being given the opportunity to identify natural inclinations, and then to decide how you want to use these inclinations as you develop your individuality.

A sign of a planet represents the potential for a psychological function in your psyche to develop a certain way of acting. This way of acting can be developed and expressed in a number of ways.

For example, an Aries way of acting can be expressed with initiative, energetically, spontaneously, aggressively, assertively, or in an overbearing and abrasive way. One individual may express this Aries way of being by choosing to initiate new projects or directions. He or she might become a leader who can inspire people into action, or an entrepreneur who starts new business ventures. Another individual may express this Aries way of being by choosing a more physically aggressive way of acting, perhaps in sports, or in a military or law enforcement career. Another individual might be expressing this Aries way of being negatively in an overbearing, abrasive way that abuses or hurts others. All come from the same Arian way of being. In Chapter 3 you learned why these ways of acting describe Aries, as well as why other ways of acting describe the other signs.

The words and phrases that you choose will depend on a number of factors, such as other psychological inclinations and potentials in your psyche, the stage of development you are in your life, and how much you have worked to understand and develop yourself. It will also depend on your environment and the opportunities and limitations you have in you life presently.

As you continue to study your birth chart and to use astrology you will be able to understand how all of these different factors in your life interrelate and how you can have control of shaping them as you want.

As you approach each psychological function (planet) in your birth chart and as you try to choose words to describe its way of acting or its focus of activity, think how you <u>want</u> to act. Try on different words just like you might try on different clothes before choosing what you want to wear. Remember, that you have the choice.

Question 2: *What if I don't like the characteristics of my Sun sign or the sign of one of my other planets?*

It is common to be more drawn to the characteristics and focuses of some signs and houses than others. I recommend that you first focus your interpretation on the signs and houses to which you feel drawn. As you use the exercises later in this book you will have the opportunity to come back and explore how you might be able to develop and integrate psychological functions, ways of acting or focuses of activity that you don't now like.

Astrology challenges us to accept and develop all sides of ourselves. However, the process of developing the different sides of our individuality takes many years, perhaps a lifetime. It is important that you don't see this process as a burden, but as an opportunity. You can accept and feel good about who you are, and yet also know you have greater potentials in yourself; potentials that you can consciously choose to develop.

Question 3: *Are some planets, signs or houses more important than others in my birth chart?*

All of the psychological functions, ways of acting, and focuses of activity symbolized by the planets, signs and houses are equally important.

The healthy, **well-rounded individual** is one who can act in whatever way the moment calls for. This means that we have the capacity to act in all of the ways symbolized by each of the signs, in all life activities symbolized by each of the houses, and with all the psychological functions symbolized by each of the planets.

Each individual has the capacity to act . . .

. . . in his/her own behalf (Aries),

. . . in consideration of others (Libra),

. . . with a focus on his/her community responsibility (10th house),

. . . with a focus on social progress and the welfare of everyone in the community (11th house),

. . . using his/her rational mind (Mercury),

. . . and using his/her receptivity to non-rational emotional perceptions of universal realities (Neptune).

Each individual is meant to continually develop his or her individuality in order to be able to function with increased effectiveness in life.

The environment in which you grew from infancy into an adult has facilitated the development of certain potentials of your individuality, and it has impeded others. The challenge for you as an adult is to develop an understanding of each of your potentials. Then you will be able to more consciously determine ways in which you want to "actualize" your potentials. Studying your birth chart allows you to gain this type of understanding.

Question 4: *Aren't the Sun and Moon considered more important than the other planets?*

All of the planets need to be recognized as important. All of the psychological functions they symbolize need to be consciously integrated within the psyche of the individual. However, the Sun and Moon are usually given more weight regardless of their positions and emphasis in the birth chart.

The Sun represents the psychological function that urges and allows you to become a unique, confident individual. The Sun's psychological function urges and allows you to develop and integrate all sides of your psyche and individuality. It represents the center of your psyche.

The Moon represents your emotional response to life on a daily basis. The Moon represents the psychological function that contains all conditioned, subconscious habit patterns and emotional defense systems. The Moon symbolizes the psychological function that is perhaps first operating in the newborn baby. It is the psychological function that indicates **how** and **where** in life we feel most emotionally satisfied and secure.

It should be noted that most individuals operate more naturally with the Moon's psychological function than with the Sun's psychological function from birth to their late 20s and even longer. Therefore, in your birth chart you need to carefully consider the relationships between your Sun and Moon positions. For example, if the ways of acting of the Sun and Moon's signs are different, it is common to feel more comfortable with your Moon sign characteristics. Usually it is the Moon sign that one can develop more easily. The Sun sign takes longer and requires more conscious effort to develop.

Question 5: *How do I know which psychological functions are more emphasized than others in my birth chart?*

One purpose of this first volume is to allow you to interpret your ten psychological functions as symbolized by the signs and house positions of the planets in your birth chart. In later volumes of this astrological series you will learn how to identify points of emphasis. However, as you use the exercises of this book you will intuitively be able to recognize some points of emphasis as you explore the signs and house positions of your planets.

Question 6: *I've heard people talk about the Rising Sign or the sign on the Ascendant. I've also head people talk about such things as, Fire, Earth, Air and Water signs, asteroids, and aspects. Will we learn about what these things mean in our birth chart?*

These astrological symbols do represent important aspects of your psyche. In later volumes of this astrological series you will have the opportunity to explore the meanings these symbols have in your birth chart.

The goal of this first volume is to explain the underlying cyclical principle on which most astrological symbolism is based and to give you the opportunity to explore what the planets in their signs and house positions mean in your birth chart.

Question 7: *Many books on astrology explain what the signs and house positions of planets mean. Wouldn't referring to these types of books be an easier way to understand what these combinations of symbols mean?*

Many astrology books that explain the meanings of the signs and house positions of planets are excellent and I recommend that you buy and refer to the ones that have meaning for you.

In this book I am attempting to give you the understanding that will allow you to develop your own interpretation of the symbolism and to better assess other people's interpretations. I am also attempting to give you exercises that will allow you to specifically relate the symbolism in your birth chart to your life.

This process does take a little more work, but I believe it will give you a more personalized interpretation of your birth chart.

Question 8: *What does it mean to study the birth chart as a whole?*

It is important to study the important parts of the birth chart as well as how the parts interrelate as a whole.

You Need to Consider Your Birth Chart as a Whole

While the birth chart allows you to analyze and understand specific parts of your self, each of these separate parts is dynamically related to the other parts. Each part is affected by the other parts. As you increase your understanding and skills in interpreting the astrological symbolism of your birth chart, you will ultimately learn to see each symbol in reference to the whole chart.

The Benefits of Analyzing Specific Symbols of Your Birth Chart

Even though part of your psychological nature operates in isolation from the whole, there are definite advantages to isolating the different sides of your self for study and analysis. You not only gain a more complete understanding of how the different sides of yourself function most naturally; you also expand your awareness of your special potentials for growth and self-actualization.

In-depth Analysis of Your Psychological Functions

Imagine looking into a microscope and seeing the expanses of the universe. By exploring the ten psychological functions of your complex psyche in detail, you will be able to identify the vast potentials each can have for you. For example, by using the exercises in this chapter you will be able to explore the ways you are naturally inclined to emotionally respond to life (Moon) and how this might be similar or different than the ways you are naturally inclined to think and communicate (Mercury). You will be able to explore how the ways you give and receive love (Venus) might be similar or different from the ways that you express your sexual drives and desires (Mars).

The exercises in this chapter will allow you to interpret the meanings of the following combinations of psychological qualities involved with each of your psychological functions:

1. **The planet's sign** (two psychological qualities), which symbolizes the psychological function's inclination to act in certain ways in order to develop specific individual potentials.

2. **The planet's house position** (two psychological qualities), which symbolizes the psychological function's inclination to focus on certain types of activities in order to develop specific individual potentials.

3. **The blend of the planet's sign and house position** (three psychological qualities). After understanding the meanings of the planet's sign and house position separately, it is necessary to understand the meaning that this **combination** of psychological qualities can have for you and the potential ways this combination can be expressed in your behavior.

As an illustration, let's look at Alice's chart (see page 7), and determine the different combinations of psychological qualities contained in her Moon in Scorpio in the Third House. This combination of symbols contains three significant relationships:

1. Moon in Scorpio

2. Moon in Third House

3. Moon in Scorpio in the Third House.

The Moon represents a certain psychological quality; Scorpio represents another psychological quality; and the Third House represents another. The placement of Moon in Scorpio in the Third House symbolizes that one part of Alice's psyche is a blend of these three qualities. When the Moon function of her psyche is expressed, it is most naturally expressed in a blend with the psychological qualities of Scorpio and the Third House. Alice has a tendency to emotionally respond to others and to life (the Moon) with an inclination to act intensely and with emotional depth in relationships (Scorpio) and with a focus on life activities that involve her education, the use of her mind and physical dexterity (Third House).

NOTE: On pages 206 to 217 are listed developmental potentials and keywords for each of the signs and houses. You will be choosing the developmental potentials and keywords from these lists to complete the sentences in this chapter. As emphasized in earlier exercises, when you read through these lists, choose the word or phrase that first "jumps out at you." There are no right or wrong choices.

You may find some sentences more difficult to complete than others. Perhaps the psychological qualities represented are incongruent or different from one another. Some potentials may be beyond your present experience and might therefore be difficult to relate to. Perhaps the symbolism represents parts of your individuality that remain in the background of your psyche. In any case, this process allows you to begin discovering these potentials for yourself. If a sentence is difficult to complete, go on to the next sentence, or even to another planet, and come back to this sentence at a later time.

Finally, I recommend that you photocopy the lists of developmental potentials and keywords found in Appendix VI. It will be easier for you to set the appropriate lists beside the sentence that you are completing rather than turning back to the appendix to review the lists.

For each planet use the following steps in your analysis:

Step 1: Note the planet's sign and house position in the designated space on the first page (cover page).

Step 2: On the next page complete the set of sentences that you have chosen with the **sign's** developmental potentials and keywords that you choose from the appropriate lists found on pages 206 to 217.

NOTE: The first sentence of the set allows you to identify the developmental potential related to the sign position. Then you are asked to complete the <u>same</u> sentence this time with a descriptive word or phrase for a way of acting or being. This has been constructed in this manner to emphasize and help you see clearly that your individual characteristics are derived from your developmental potentials. You are inclined to act in a certain manner in order to become more developed, evolved or improved in that way of acting.

EXAMPLE:

Moon in Leo

I am inclined to feel the most satisfied emotionally in a way that will develop

my personal, unique creativity.
_____
(developmental potential)

Therefore:

I am inclined to feel the most satisfied by acting

self-expressively, with a need for attention, dramatically,
(egotistically, self-centeredly).
_____
(keywords for sign)

Step 3: On the bottom half of the same page you can make notes in the space provided as you interpret the positive and negative potentials related to the planet's sign position. The idea here is to "brainstorm" positive and negative potentials regardless of whether they describe you.

Step 4: On the next page (3rd page) analyze the planet's house position. Follow the same recommendations given in Step 1.

NOTE: The wording of this set of sentences is the same as the sentences used to analyze the planet's sign position, except that the endings of the sentences are different to reflect the symbolism of the planet's house position. Instead of the ending, "by acting in a way that will develop," it is "by focusing on activities that will develop."

EXAMPLE:

Moon in 8th House

I am inclined to feel the most satisfied emotionally by focusing on activities that will develop

my ability to be an emotionally sharing individual.
_____
(developmental potential)

therefore:

I am inclined to feel the most satisfied emotionally focusing on

losing my sense of separateness in a relationship,
psychological transformations, intimacy.
_____
(keywords for house)

Step 5: On the bottom half of the same page you can make notes in the space provided as you interpret the positive and negative potentials related to the planet's **house** position. Again, you are meant to "brainstorm" positive and negative potentials regardless of whether or not they describe you at this time.

Step 6: Read through the four sentences on the next page (4th page). The focus here is on analyzing the **combination of the planet's sign and house position.**

Complete these sentences with keywords for both the planet's sign and house positions. These sentences will allow you to interpret the meaning of the combination of these psychological qualities. Each planet represents a psychological function in your psyche that focuses on a certain type of activity (house), with an urge to act in a certain way, with certain characteristics (sign). These three qualities have to be considered as affecting each other and blending together for you to obtain a fuller understanding of how the psychological function is naturally inclined to operate in your daily life.

NOTE: In steps 2 and 3, you explored the meaning of the sign of the planet and in steps 4 and 5 you explored the meaning of the house position of the planet. In step 6, to be able to explore the meaning of the combination of the sign and house position of the planet, you are asked to first fill in the blank related to the planet's house position and then complete the blank related to the planet's sign position. The reason you are asked to complete the blanks in this order has to do with the grammatical correctness and readability of the sentence.

EXAMPLE:

Moon in 8th House in Leo.

I am inclined to feel the most satisfied by focusing on

Activity (House Position)	Way(s) of Acting (Sign Position)
intimacy	*self-expressively, romantically (self-centeredly).*
sharing resources	*creatively (domineeringly).*
emotional risk-taking	*self-assuredly, confidently.*

NOTE: I have included additional sentences for you to complete so that you can explore the different ways each psychological function can be used by you. However, you may want to analyze only one sentence the first time you approach this interpretive exercise. If you try to complete the blanks of all the sentences in one sitting too many words and concepts may become confusing. I also recommend that the first sentence you analyze be the same one that you have been working with on the previous pages.

Step 6: Make notes on the opposite page (5th page). The questions provided on this page are designed to assist you in determining the positive potentials that already exist in your individuality, the new potentials you want to develop and the negative behavior patterns you want to overcome.

Step 7: On the final page (6th page) space has been provided for you to make further notes based on your analysis and interpretation. You can use this space to define short-term and long-term goals to actualize the positive potentials that are related to the psychological function you want to develop. You can also use this space to complete sentences with different developmental potentials and keywords.

In Appendix III I have discussed in depth the method for analyzing astrological symbolism that relates to questions and worksheets in this section. I recommend that you read through Appendix III before you begin your analysis.

Advanced Interpretive Consideration

To be able to use the following interpretative consideration you will need to have read Appendix II (How To Read A Birth Chart Form), and know what "cusps" of signs and planets are.

When a planet is within three to five degrees of the next sign you need to consider the planet in both signs. Also when a planet is within three to five degrees of the next house you need to consider the planet in both houses.

For example, in Alice's birth chart she has the Moon and Saturn four degrees from the third house. Therefore, the psychological functions that these planets represent will be affected by the psychological qualities symbolized by both 3rd and 4th houses.

In Appendix IV I interpret the planets in Alice's birth chart that are near cusps of signs and houses.

MERCURY

Capacity To Think
and Communicate Rationally

Mercury Sign Position   ♋ *Cancer* _____

Mercury House Position _____ *11th House* _____

Mercury Sign Position ♋ *Cancer*

I am inclined to use my rational thinking function in a way that will develop

my personal sense of emotional security.

(developmental potential)

therefore:

I am inclined to use my rational thinking function by acting

caringly, responsively (insecurely, defensively).

(key words for sign)

Interpreting Your Mercury Sign Position

Now that you have completed these sentences you can use the space below to explore the positive and negative potentials of this combination of psychological qualities.

Rational thinking and emotional needs may be incompatible. Emotions might interfere with rational objectivity and logic.

Positive — Ability to mentally perceive emotional needs of self and others.

Negative — Insecurities and emotional subjective thinking could interfere with my rational thinking. Could be defensive and shy about communicating my needs to others.

Mercury House Position ___ 11th House

I am inclined to use my rational thinking function by focusing on activities that will develop

my progressive, futuristic, inventive thinking abilities.

therefore:

I am inclined to use my rational thinking function by focusing on

creative, symbolic expression on mental levels. Experimenting.

(key words for house)

Interpreting Your Mercury House Position

Now that you have completed these sentences you can use the space below to explore the positive and negative potentials of this combination of psychological qualities.

Positive — Mentally open to new ideas. Symbolic thinking useful in art, science and perhaps community-oriented activities.

Negative — If logical, rational mind not well-developed, I might be drawn to activities involving experimental ideas that are not well thought out.

Mercury – Blending Signs And House Positions

1. I am inclined to use my rational thinking function by focusing on

creative, symbolic thinking   *imaginatively.*

futuristic, inventive thinking   *with emotional clarity.*

_____

      ACTIVITY (HOUSE POSITION)   WAY(S) OF ACTING (SIGN POSITION)

2. I am inclined to communicate with others by focusing on

social causes   *nurturingly, responsively.*

mass communications   *caringly, sensitively.*

_____

      ACTIVITY (HOUSE POSITION)   WAY(S) OF ACTING (SIGN POSITION)

3. I am inclined to examine and analyze information by focusing on

_____

_____

      ACTIVITY (HOUSE POSITION)   WAY(S) OF ACTING (SIGN POSITION)

4. I am inclined to use my rational, logical mind by focusing on

_____

_____

      ACTIVITY (HOUSE POSITION)   WAY(S) OF ACTING (SIGN POSITION)

Actualizing Your Potential –
Mercury Sign/House Blend

1. Identify the positive potentials of this psychological energy combination that you recognize now exist in your individuality.

While I value rational thought, the emotional needs of myself and others are important to me. I use my "emotional thinking" when I play the piano and write music (symbolic, creative expressions).

2. Determine which of these existing positive potentials that you want to develop further or use in new ways. Define in what new ways.

I want to focus on helping others in a humanitarian way, but also in a personal and nurturing manner. I want to use my attunement to emotional needs to film personal stories of other people (making mass media more personally oriented).

3. Choose new positive potentials of this psychological energy combination that you want to activate.

Using my ability to think and communicate in humanitarian areas of life and in a way that I can be nurturing to others.

4. Identify negative behavior patterns associated with this combination of qualities that you want to overcome.

I still need to be more objective about other peoples thoughts and emotional needs. I tend to be rather subjective in my thinking.

Goal Setting/Notes/Themes

1. Follow-up on my interests to join the Peace Corps.

2. Make notes on creating videos that will reflect poetic, emotional needs of others. Write music for these videos.

3. Continue to explore ways to become more objective about my feelings. Perhaps start a journal.

SUN

$\odot$

Capacity
To Become An Individual

Sun Sign Position _____

Sun House Position _____

Sun Sign Position _____

I am inclined to express my individuality in a way that will develop

_____

(developmental potential)

therefore:

I am inclined to express my individuality by acting

_____

(key words for sign)

Interpreting Your Sun Sign Position

Now that you have completed these sentences you can use the space below to explore the positive and negative potentials of this combination of psychological qualities.

_____
_____
_____
_____
_____
_____
_____
_____
_____
_____
_____
_____
_____
_____
_____
_____
_____
_____

Sun House Position _____

I am inclined to express my individuality by focusing on activities that will develop

_____

(developmental potential)

therefore:

I am inclined to express my individuality by focusing on

_____

(key words for house)

Interpreting Your Sun House Position

Now that you have completed these sentences you can use the space below to explore the positive and negative potentials of this combination of psychological qualities.

_____
_____
_____
_____
_____
_____
_____
_____
_____
_____
_____
_____
_____
_____
_____
_____
_____
_____

Sun – Blending Signs And House Positions

1. I am inclined to express my individuality by focusing on

_____

_____

ACTIVITY (HOUSE POSITION)   WAY(S) OF ACTING (SIGN POSITION).

2. I am inclined to be self-expressive and creative by focusing on

_____

_____

ACTIVITY (HOUSE POSITION)   WAY(S) OF ACTING (SIGN POSITION)

3. I am inclined to express my unique vitality by focusing on

_____

_____

ACTIVITY (HOUSE POSITION)   WAY(S) OF ACTING (SIGN POSITION)

4. I am inclined to express my urge to become an individual by focusing on

_____

_____

ACTIVITY (HOUSE POSITION)   WAY(S) OF ACTING (SIGN POSITION)

Astrology for the Absolute Beginner

Actualizing Your Potential –
Sun Sign/House Blend

1. Identify the positive potentials of this energy combination that you recognize now exist in your individuality.

_____

_____

_____

_____

2. Determine which of these existing positive potentials that you want to develop further or use in new ways. Define in what new ways.

_____

_____

_____

_____

3. Choose new positive potentials of this energy combination that you want to activate.

_____

_____

_____

_____

4. Identify negative behavior patterns associated with this combination of qualities that you want to overcome.

_____

_____

_____

_____

Goal Setting/Notes/Themes

MOON

☽

Capacity
For Emotional Expression

Moon Sign Position _____

Moon House Position _____

Moon Sign Position _____

I am inclined to feel the most satisfied emotionally by acting in a way that will develop

_____

(developmental potential)

therefore:

I am inclined to feel the most satisfied by acting

_____

(key words for sign)

Interpreting Your Moon Sign Position

Now that you have completed these sentences you can use the space below to explore the positive and negative potentials of this combination of psychological qualities.

_____
_____
_____
_____
_____
_____
_____
_____
_____
_____
_____
_____
_____
_____
_____
_____
_____

Moon House Position

I am inclined to feel most satisfied emotionally by focusing on activities that will develop

_____

(developmental potential)

therefore:

I am inclined to feel the most satisfied emotionally by focusing on

_____

(key words for house)

Interpreting Your Moon House Position

Now that you have completed these sentences you can use the space below to explore the positive and negative potentials of this combination of psychological qualities.

_____

_____

_____

_____

_____

_____

_____

_____

_____

_____

_____

_____

_____

_____

_____

_____

_____

_____

_____

Moon – Blending Signs And House Positions

1. I am inclined to feel the most satisfied emotionally by focusing on

_____

_____

_____

      ACTIVITY (HOUSE POSITION)   WAY(S) OF ACTING (SIGN POSITION)

2. I am inclined to emotionally respond to life by focusing on

_____

_____

_____

      ACTIVITY (HOUSE POSITION)   WAY(S) OF ACTING (SIGN POSITION)

3. I am inclined to seek feelings of emotional security and well-being by focusing on

_____

_____

_____

      ACTIVITY (HOUSE POSITION)   WAY(S) OF ACTING (SIGN POSITION)

4. I am inclined to express my emotional nature by focusing on

_____

_____

_____

      ACTIVITY (HOUSE POSITION)   WAY(S) OF ACTING (SIGN POSITION)

Actualizing Your Potential –
Moon Sign/House Blend

1. Identify the positive potentials of this energy combination that you recognize now exist in your individuality.

   _____

   _____

   _____

   _____

   _____

2. Determine which of these existing positive potentials that you want to develop further or use in new ways. Define in what new ways.

   _____

   _____

   _____

   _____

   _____

3. Choose new positive potentials of this energy combination that you want to activate.

   _____

   _____

   _____

   _____

   _____

4. Identify negative behavior patterns associated with this combination of qualities that you want to overcome.

   _____

   _____

   _____

   _____

   _____

Goal Setting/Notes/Themes

MERCURY

*Capacity to Think
and Communicate Rationally*

Mercury Sign Position _____

Mercury House Position _____

Mercury Sign Position _____

I am inclined to use my rational thinking function in a way that will develop

_____

(developmental potential)

therefore:

I am inclined to use my rational thinking function by acting

_____

(key words for sign)

Interpreting Your Mercury Sign Position

Now that you have completed these sentences you can use the space below to explore the positive and negative potentials of this combination of psychological qualities.

_____
_____
_____
_____
_____
_____
_____
_____
_____
_____
_____
_____
_____
_____
_____
_____

Mercury House Position _____

I am inclined to use my rational thinking function by focusing on activities that will develop

_____

(developmental potential)

therefore:

I am inclined to use my rational thinking function by focusing on

_____

(key words for house)

Interpreting Mercury House Position

Now that you have completed these sentences you can use the space below to explore the positive and negative potentials of this combination of psychological qualities.

_____

_____

_____

_____

_____

_____

_____

_____

_____

_____

_____

_____

_____

_____

_____

_____

_____

_____

_____

Mercury — Blending Signs And House Positions

1. I am inclined to use my rational thinking function by focusing on

_____

_____

_____

    ACTIVITY (HOUSE POSITION)   WAY(S) OF ACTING (SIGN POSITION)

2. I am inclined to communicate with others by focusing on

_____

_____

_____

    ACTIVITY (HOUSE POSITION)   WAY(S) OF ACTING (SIGN POSITION)

3. I am inclined to examine and analyze information by focusing on

_____

_____

_____

    ACTIVITY (HOUSE POSITION)   WAY(S) OF ACTING (SIGN POSITION)

4. I am inclined to use my rational, logical mind by focusing on

_____

_____

_____

    ACTIVITY (HOUSE POSITION)   WAY(S) OF ACTING (SIGN POSITION)

Actualizing Your Potential –
Mercury Sign/House Blend

1. Identify the positive potentials of this energy combination that you recognize now exist in your individuality.

_____

_____

_____

_____

_____

2. Determine which of these existing positive potentials that you want to develop further or use in new ways. Define in what new ways.

_____

_____

_____

_____

_____

3. Choose new positive potentials of this energy combination that you want to activate.

_____

_____

_____

_____

_____

4. Identify negative behavior patterns associated with this combination of qualities that you want to overcome.

_____

_____

_____

_____

Goal Setting/Notes/Themes

VENUS

♀

Capacity For Social Receptivity
Capacity For Sensual Receptivity

Venus Sign Position _____

Venus House Position _____

Venus Sign Position _____

I am inclined to give and receive love in a way that will develop

_____

(developmental potential)

therefore:

I am inclined to give and receive love by acting

_____

(key words for sign)

Interpreting Your Venus Sign Position

Now that you have completed these sentences you can use the space below to explore the positive and negative potentials of this combination of psychological qualities.

_____
_____
_____
_____
_____
_____
_____
_____
_____
_____
_____
_____
_____
_____
_____
_____
_____

Venus House Position _____

I am inclined to give and receive love by focusing on activities that will develop

_____

(developmental potential)

therefore:

I am inclined to give and receive love by focusing on

_____

(key words for house)

Interpreting Your Venus House Position

Now that you have completed these sentences you can use the space below to explore the positive and negative potentials of this combination of psychological qualities.

_____
_____
_____
_____
_____
_____
_____
_____
_____
_____
_____
_____
_____
_____
_____
_____
_____
_____
_____

Venus – Blending Signs And House Positions

1. I am inclined to give and receive love by focusing on

_____

_____

_____

ACTIVITY (HOUSE POSITION)   WAY(S) OF ACTING (SIGN POSITION)

2. I am inclined to express my likes, dislikes, and values by focusing on

_____

_____

_____

ACTIVITY (HOUSE POSITION)   WAY(S) OF ACTING (SIGN POSITION)

3. I am inclined to satisfy my sensual and physical needs by focusing on

_____

_____

_____

ACTIVITY (HOUSE POSITION)   WAY(S) OF ACTING (SIGN POSITION)

4. I am inclined to express my social nature by focusing on

_____

_____

_____

ACTIVITY (HOUSE POSITION)   WAY(S) OF ACTING (SIGN POSITION)

Actualizing Your Potential –
Venus Sign/House Blend

1. Identify the positive potentials of this energy combination that you recognize now exist in your individuality.

   _____

   _____

   _____

   _____

   _____

2. Determine which of these existing positive potentials that you want to develop further or use in new ways. Define in what new ways.

   _____

   _____

   _____

   _____

   _____

3. Choose new positive potentials of this energy combination that you want to activate.

   _____

   _____

   _____

   _____

   _____

4. Identify negative behavior patterns associated with this combination of qualities that you want to overcome.

   _____

   _____

   _____

   _____

Goal Setting/Notes/Themes

MARS

Capacity To Be Assertive

Mars Sign Position _____

Mars House Position _____

Mars Sign Position _____

I am inclined to be energetic on my own behalf in a way that will develop

_____

(developmental potential)

therefore:

I am inclined to be energetic on my own behalf by acting

_____

(key words for sign)

Interpreting Your Mars Sign Position

Now that you have completed these sentences you can use the space below to explore the positive and negative potentials of this combination of psychological qualities.

_____
_____
_____
_____
_____
_____
_____
_____
_____
_____
_____
_____
_____
_____
_____
_____
_____
_____
_____
_____
_____

Mars House Position _____

I am inclined to be energetic on my own behalf in a way that will develop

_____

(developmental potential)

therefore:

I am inclined to be energetic on my own behalf by focusing on

_____

(key words for house)

Interpreting Your Mars House Position

Now that you have completed these sentences you can use the space below to explore the positive and negative potentials of this combination of psychological qualities.

_____

_____

_____

_____

_____

_____

_____

_____

_____

_____

_____

_____

_____

_____

_____

_____

_____

_____

_____

Mars — Blending Signs And House Positions

1. I am inclined to be energetic on my own behalf by focusing on

_____

_____

_____

      ACTIVITY (HOUSE POSITION)   WAY(S) OF ACTING (SIGN POSITION)

2. I am inclined to express my sexual drives and desires by focusing on

_____

_____

_____

      ACTIVITY (HOUSE POSITION)   WAY(S) OF ACTING (SIGN POSITION)

3. I am inclined to express my anger by focusing on

_____

_____

_____

      ACTIVITY (HOUSE POSITION)   WAY(S) OF ACTING (SIGN POSITION)

4. I am inclined to be assertive by focusing on

_____

_____

_____

      ACTIVITY (HOUSE POSITION)   WAY(S) OF ACTING (SIGN POSITION)

Actualizing Your Potential – Mars Sign/House Blend

1. Identify the positive potentials of this energy combination that you recognize now exist in your individuality.

_____

_____

_____

_____

_____

2. Determine which of these existing positive potentials that you want to develop further or use in new ways. Define in what new ways.

_____

_____

_____

_____

_____

3. Choose new positive potentials of this energy combination that you want to activate.

_____

_____

_____

_____

_____

4. Identify negative behavior patterns associated with this combination of qualities that you want to overcome.

_____

_____

_____

_____

Goal Setting/Notes/Themes

JUPITER

4

Capacities For Expansion
And Abstract Thinking

Jupiter Sign Position _____

Jupiter House Position _____

Jupiter Sign Position _____

I am inclined to seek opportunities for social and mental growth in a way that will develop

_____

(developmental potential)

therefore:

I am inclined to opportunities for social and mental growth by acting

_____

(key words for sign)

Interpreting Your Jupiter Sign Position

Now that you have completed these sentences you can use the space below to explore the positive and negative potentials of this combination of psychological qualities.

_____

_____

_____

_____

_____

_____

_____

_____

_____

_____

_____

_____

_____

_____

_____

_____

_____

_____

Jupiter House Position _____

I am inclined to seek opportunities for social and mental growth by focusing on activities that will develop

_____

(developmental potential)

therefore:

I am inclined to seek opportunities for social and mental growth by focusing on

_____

(key words for house)

Interpreting Your Jupiter House Position

Now that you have completed these sentences you can use the space below to explore the positive and negative potentials of this combination of psychological qualities.

_____
_____
_____
_____
_____
_____
_____
_____
_____
_____
_____
_____
_____
_____
_____
_____
_____
_____

Jupiter – Blending Signs And House Positions

1. I am inclined to seek opportunities for social and mental growth by focusing on

_____

_____

_____

     ACTIVITY (HOUSE POSITION)   WAY(S) OF ACTING (SIGN POSITION)

2. I am inclined to seek ideas for my belief system by focusing on

_____

_____

_____

     ACTIVITY (HOUSE POSITION)   WAY(S) OF ACTING (SIGN POSITION)

3. I am inclined to explore new horizons by focusing on

_____

_____

_____

     ACTIVITY (HOUSE POSITION)   WAY(S) OF ACTING (SIGN POSITION)

4. I am inclined to be expand beyond my circumstances in life by focusing on

_____

_____

_____

     ACTIVITY (HOUSE POSITION)   WAY(S) OF ACTING (SIGN POSITION)

Actualizing Your Potential –
Jupiter Sign/House Blend

1. Identify the positive potentials of this energy combination that you recognize now exist in your individuality.

_____

_____

_____

_____

_____

2. Determine which of these existing positive potentials that you want to develop further or use in new ways. Define in what new ways.

_____

_____

_____

_____

_____

3. Choose new positive potentials of this energy combination that you want to activate.

_____

_____

_____

_____

_____

4. Identify negative behavior patterns associated with this combination of qualities that you want to overcome.

_____

_____

_____

_____

_____

Goal Setting/Notes/Themes

_____

_____

_____

_____

_____

_____

_____

_____

_____

_____

_____

_____

_____

_____

_____

_____

_____

_____

_____

_____

_____

_____

_____

_____

_____

_____

_____

_____

_____

_____

_____

_____

SATURN

♄

Capacities For Self-Discipline And Maturity

Saturn Sign Position _____

Saturn House Position _____

Saturn Sign Position _____

I am inclined to handle difficult life tests and challenges in a way that will develop

_____

(developmental potential)

therefore:

I am inclined to handle difficult life tests and challenges by acting

_____

(key words for sign)

Interpreting Your Saturn Sign Position

Now that you have completed these sentences you can use the space below to explore the positive and negative potentials of this combination of psychological qualities.

_____
_____
_____
_____
_____
_____
_____
_____
_____
_____
_____
_____
_____
_____
_____
_____
_____
_____
_____

Saturn House Position _____

I am inclined to handle difficult life tests and challenges by focusing on activities that will develop

_____

(developmental potential)

therefore:

I am inclined to handle difficult life tests and challenges by focusing on

_____

(key words for house)

Interpreting Your Saturn House Position

Now that you have completed these sentences you can use the space below to explore the positive and negative potentials of this combination of psychological qualities.

_____
_____
_____
_____
_____
_____
_____
_____
_____
_____
_____
_____
_____
_____
_____
_____
_____
_____

Saturn – Blending Signs And House Positions

1. I am inclined to handle difficult life tests and challenges by focusing on

_____

_____

_____

    ACTIVITY (HOUSE POSITION)   WAY(S) OF ACTING (SIGN POSITION)

2. I am inclined to organize and structure life by focusing on

_____

_____

_____

    ACTIVITY (HOUSE POSITION)   WAY(S) OF ACTING (SIGN POSITION)

3. I am inclined to handle self-doubt from others' judgments by focusing on

_____

_____

_____

    ACTIVITY (HOUSE POSITION)   WAY(S) OF ACTING (SIGN POSITION)

4. I am inclined to be responsible and self-disciplined by focusing on

_____

_____

_____

    ACTIVITY (HOUSE POSITION)   WAY(S) OF ACTING (SIGN POSITION)

Actualizing Your Potential –
Saturn Sign/House Blend

1. Identify the positive potentials of this energy combination that you recognize now exist in your individuality.

_____

_____

_____

_____

_____

2. Determine which of these existing positive potentials that you want to develop further or use in new ways. Define in what new ways.

_____

_____

_____

_____

_____

3. Choose new positive potentials of this energy combination that you want to activate.

_____

_____

_____

_____

_____

4. Identify negative behavior patterns associated with this combination of qualities that you want to overcome.

_____

_____

_____

_____

Goal Setting/Notes/Themes

URANUS

♅

Capacity For Higher Mental, Intuitive Thinking

Uranus Sign Position _____

Uranus House Position _____

Uranus Sign Position _____

I am inclined to think of new, progressive, creative ideas in a way that will develop

_____

(developmental potential)

therefore:

I am inclined to think of new, progressive, creative ideas by acting

_____

(key words for sign)

Interpreting Your Uranus Sign Position

Now that you have completed these sentences you can use the space below to explore the positive and negative potentials of this combination of psychological qualities.

_____
_____
_____
_____
_____
_____
_____
_____
_____
_____
_____
_____
_____
_____
_____
_____
_____
_____
_____

Uranus House Position _____

I am inclined to think of new, progressive, creative ideas by focusing on activities that will develop

_____

(developmental potential)

therefore:

I am inclined to think of new, progressive, creative ideas by focusing on

_____

(key words for house)

Interpreting Your Uranus House Position

Now that you have completed these sentences you can use the space below to explore the positive and negative potentials of this combination of psychological qualities.

_____
_____
_____
_____
_____
_____
_____
_____
_____
_____
_____
_____
_____
_____
_____
_____
_____
_____
_____

Uranus – Blending Signs And House Positions

1. I am inclined to think of new, progressive, creative ideas by focusing on

_____

_____

_____

    ACTIVITY (HOUSE POSITION)   WAY(S) OF ACTING (SIGN POSITION)

2. I am inclined to use my intuitive perceptions of future possibilities by focusing on

_____

_____

_____

    ACTIVITY (HOUSE POSITION)   WAY(S) OF ACTING (SIGN POSITION)

3. I am inclined to change outdated ideas and expectations by focusing on

_____

_____

_____

    ACTIVITY (HOUSE POSITION)   WAY(S) OF ACTING (SIGN POSITION)

4. I am inclined to use my higher, inventive mind by focusing on

_____

_____

_____

    ACTIVITY (HOUSE POSITION)   WAY(S) OF ACTING (SIGN POSITION)

Actualizing Your Potential —
Uranus Sign/House Blend

1. Identify the positive potentials of this energy combination that you recognize now exist in your individuality.

   _____

   _____

   _____

   _____

   _____

2. Determine which of these existing positive potentials that you want to develop further or use in new ways. Define in what new ways.

   _____

   _____

   _____

   _____

   _____

3. Choose new positive potentials of this energy combination that you want to activate.

   _____

   _____

   _____

   _____

   _____

4. Identify negative behavior patterns associated with this combination of qualities that you want to overcome.

   _____

   _____

   _____

   _____

Goal Setting/Notes/Themes

_____
_____
_____
_____
_____
_____
_____
_____
_____
_____
_____
_____
_____
_____
_____
_____
_____
_____
_____
_____
_____
_____
_____
_____
_____
_____
_____
_____
_____
_____
_____
_____
_____
_____
_____

NEPTUNE

Ψ

Capacity To Be Receptive
To Dreams, Inspirations And Visions

Neptune Sign Position _____

Neptune House Position _____

Neptune Sign Position

I am inclined to express my universal imagination and psychic awareness in a way that will develop

_____

(developmental potential)

therefore:

I am inclined to express my universal imagination and psychic awareness by acting

_____

(key words for sign)

Interpreting Your Neptune Sign Position

Now that you have completed these sentences you can use the space below to explore the positive and negative potentials of this combination of psychological qualities.

_____
_____
_____
_____
_____
_____
_____
_____
_____
_____
_____
_____
_____
_____
_____
_____
_____
_____

Neptune House Position

I am inclined to express my universal imagination and psychic awareness by focusing on activities that will develop

_____

(developmental potential)

therefore:

I am inclined to express my universal imagination and psychic awareness by focusing on

_____

(key words for house)

Interpreting Your Neptune House Position

Now that you have completed these sentences you can use the space below to explore the positive and negative potentials of this combination of psychological qualities.

_____

_____

_____

_____

_____

_____

_____

_____

_____

_____

_____

_____

_____

_____

_____

_____

_____

_____

_____

Neptune – Blending Signs And House Positions

1. I am inclined to express my universal imagination and psychic awareness by focusing on

_____

_____

_____

    ACTIVITY (HOUSE POSITION)   WAY(S) OF ACTING (SIGN POSITION)

2. I am inclined to express the feelings of universal oneness, compassion and empathy by focusing on

_____

_____

_____

    ACTIVITY (HOUSE POSITION)   WAY(S) OF ACTING (SIGN POSITION)

3. I am inclined to be open to other dimensions and alternate realities by focusing on

_____

_____

_____

    ACTIVITY (HOUSE POSITION)   WAY(S) OF ACTING (SIGN POSITION)

4. I am inclined to use my higher, universal emotional nature by focusing on

_____

_____

_____

    ACTIVITY (HOUSE POSITION)   WAY(S) OF ACTING (SIGN POSITION)

Actualizing Your Potential –
Neptune Sign/House Blend

1. Identify the positive potentials of this energy combination that you recognize now exist in your individuality.

   _____

   _____

   _____

   _____

   _____

2. Determine which of these existing positive potentials that you want to develop further or use in new ways. Define in what new ways.

   _____

   _____

   _____

   _____

3. Choose new positive potentials of this energy combination that you want to activate.

   _____

   _____

   _____

   _____

4. Identify negative behavior patterns associated with this combination of qualities that you want to overcome.

   _____

   _____

   _____

   _____

Goal Setting/Notes/Themes

_____

_____

_____

_____

_____

_____

_____

_____

_____

_____

_____

_____

_____

_____

_____

_____

_____

_____

_____

_____

_____

_____

_____

_____

_____

_____

_____

_____

_____

_____

_____

_____

PLUTO

♇

Capacity
For Psychological Transformation

Pluto Sign Position _____

Pluto House Position _____

Pluto Sign Position

I am inclined to transform and elevate my negatively selfish drives in a way that will develop

_____

(developmental potential)

therefore:

I am inclined to transform and elevate my negatively selfish drives by acting

_____

(key words for sign)

Interpreting Your Pluto Sign Position

Now that you have completed these sentences you can use the space below to explore the positive and negative potentials of this combination of psychological qualities.

_____
_____
_____
_____
_____
_____
_____
_____
_____
_____
_____
_____
_____
_____
_____
_____
_____
_____

Pluto House Position

I am inclined to transform and elevate my negatively selfish drives by focusing on activities that will develop

_____

(developmental potential)

therefore:

I am inclined to transform and elevate my negatively selfish drives by focusing on

_____

(key words for house)

Interpreting Your Pluto House Position

Now that you have completed these sentences you can use the space below to explore the positive and negative potentials of this combination of psychological qualities.

_____
_____
_____
_____
_____
_____
_____
_____
_____
_____
_____
_____
_____
_____
_____
_____

Pluto – Blending Signs And House Positions

1. I am inclined to transform and elevate my negatively selfish drives by focusing on

_____

_____

    ACTIVITY (HOUSE POSITION)   WAY(S) OF ACTING (SIGN POSITION)

2. I am inclined to consciously face and integrate the "dark" unaccepted sides of myself by focusing on

_____

_____

    ACTIVITY (HOUSE POSITION)   WAY(S) OF ACTING (SIGN POSITION)

3. I am inclined to passionately lose myself in a loving relationship by focusing on

_____

_____

    ACTIVITY (HOUSE POSITION)   WAY(S) OF ACTING (SIGN POSITION)

4. I am inclined to express my capacity for psychological transformation by focusing on

_____

_____

    ACTIVITY (HOUSE POSITION)   WAY(S) OF ACTING (SIGN POSITION)

Actualizing Your Potential – Pluto Sign/House Blend

1. Identify the positive potentials of this energy combination that you recognize now exist in your individuality.

_____

_____

_____

_____

_____

2. Determine which of these existing positive potentials that you want to develop further or use in new ways. Define in what new ways.

_____

_____

_____

_____

_____

3. Choose new positive potentials of this energy combination that you want to activate.

_____

_____

_____

_____

_____

4. Identify negative behavior patterns associated with this combination of qualities that you want to overcome.

_____

_____

_____

_____

Goal Setting/Notes/Themes

Appendix I
Purchasing Your
Computerized Birth Chart

In most major cities today you will be able to find astrologers who will be able to calculate and print your computerized birth chart inexpensively ($3-$7).

If you want to contact me for your computerized chart, please call 1-800-300-7439, or write Breakthrough Astrological Services, P.O. Box 5511, Eugene, OR, 97405. The cost is $5.00 plus $2.00 handling charge, and I will send you a list of the other computerized services and interpretative reports that I offer.

You will need to provide your birth date, your exact birth time, and your birth place. Do not rely on the memory of your family members, if at all possible. Check your birth certificate to see if the time of birth is recorded.

If you do not know your exact birth time, you can have a solar birth chart calculated which will give your sign positions of the planets in your birth chart, but not their house positions. Using only the sign positions of your planets can still give you valuable knowledge about your natural inclinations and developmental potentials.

If you do know the exact time of your birth, I recommend that you tell the astrological computer service to calculate your birth chart using the Placidus house system. There are a number of different house systems, but Placidus is one of the most commonly used.

Appendix II
How To Read
Your Birth Chart

The birth chart is a two-dimensional symbol of the solar system seen from earth. The first two diagrams below show the signs and houses as two separate cycles, each divided into twelve phases. The third diagram shows these cycles superimposed over each other in the birth chart. This appendix provides an introductory explanation of how these cycles are related to each other and also how the cycles of the planets are represented in the birth chart.

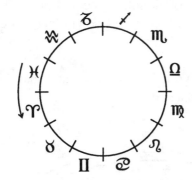

The Cycle of the Seasons

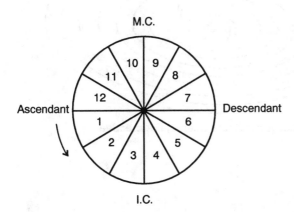

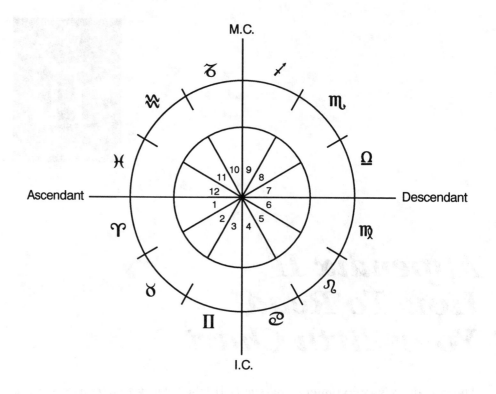

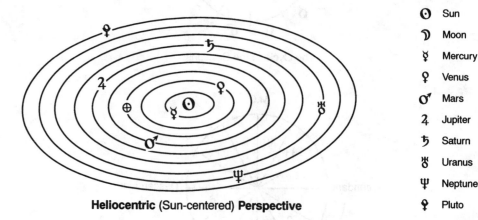

The Birth Chart Symbolizes The Solar System from Earth's Viewpoint

Even though the solar system is sun-centered, most astrological symbolism is based on the relationship of the solar system to earth. Therefore, the birth chart is diagrammed from an earth-centered viewpoint (geocentric) rather than from a sun-centered viewpoint (heliocentric).

A heliocentric perspective is based on the fact that the planets of our solar system revolve around the sun:

☉	Sun
☽	Moon
☿	Mercury
♀	Venus
♂	Mars
♃	Jupiter
♄	Saturn
♅	Uranus
♆	Neptune
♇	Pluto

figure 19

Heliocentric (Sun-centered) Perspective

The geocentric perspective symbolically places the earth at the center of our solar system. This perspective allows us to give meaning to and relate the cycles of the solar system to our lives on earth.

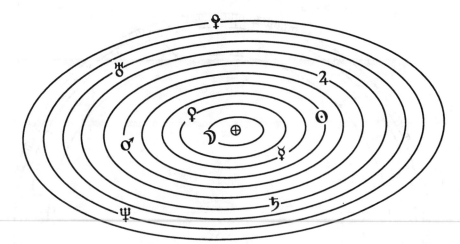

Geocentric (Earth-centered) **Perspective**

figure 20

If a person is standing in a location in the northern hemisphere on earth facing the equator, the sun appears to rise from the East and set in the West. The sun appears to revolve around the earth. This cycle that the sun appears to make around the earth in a year is referred to as the **ecliptic** and forms the basis of the tropical zodiac. Modern western astrology is based on dividing the tropical zodiac into 12 equal phases:

The Tropical Zodiac and the Ecliptic

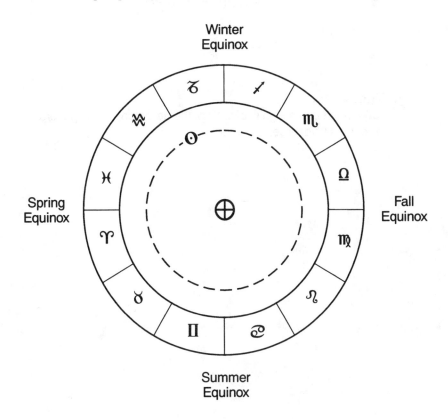

figure 21

Degrees of the Tropical Zodiac

The tropical zodiac is divided into 360 degrees. Each of the twelve signs contains 30 degrees:

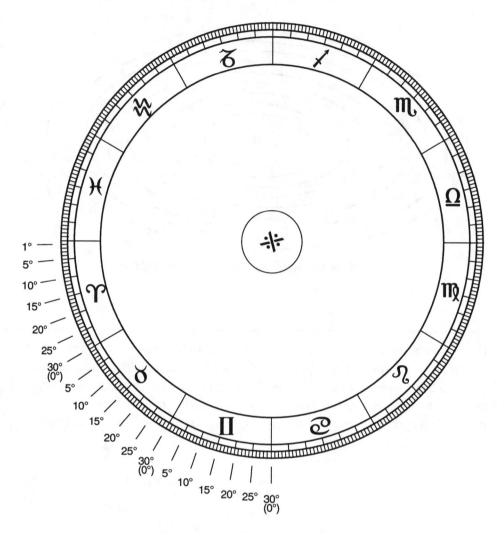

figure 22

12 Signs x 30°= 360°
The 30th degree of a sign is also 0° of the next sign, and is generally referred to as 0° degree.

As the planets proceed through their cycles, their positions are measured in terms of the degrees of the tropical zodiac. The following diagram displays Alice's planets in the exact degree (°) and minutes (') of their signs positions:

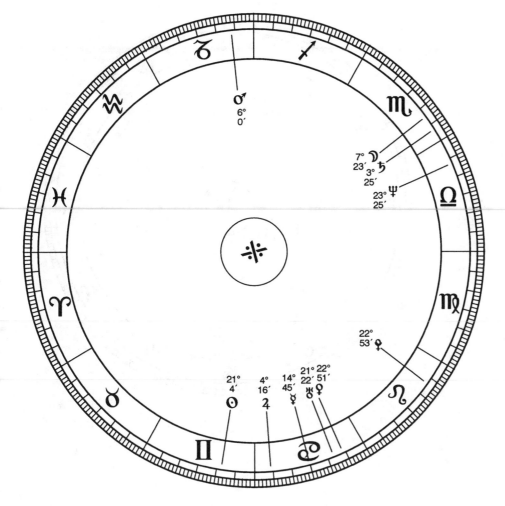

figure 23

The key to understanding astrological symbolism is learning how to relate the cycle of the day and night (houses), the cycle of the seasons (signs) and planetary cycles to each other. The houses in the birth chart provide the necessary earth-centered frame of reference to which all of the other cycles are related.

When a birth chart is calculated, the exact moment in time and the exact longitude and latitude of the birth place are used to determine the degree and minute of the sign that appears on the sunrise point of the horizon. In the sample chart below, 16 degrees, 15 minutes Scorpio was on the sunrise point of the horizon:

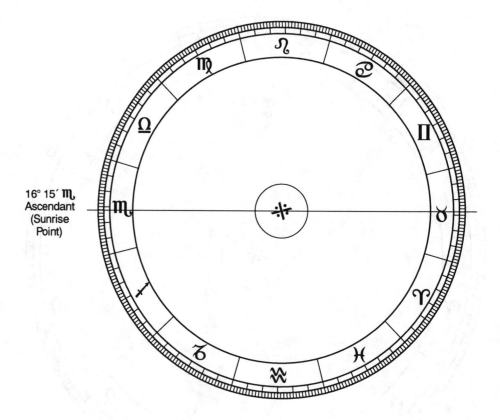

16° 15′ ♏︎
Ascendant
(Sunrise
Point)

figure 24

Astrologers use different systems to calculate the twelve house divisions. The diagram below displays the twelve houses calculated for Alice's chart, using the most common house system (Placidus):

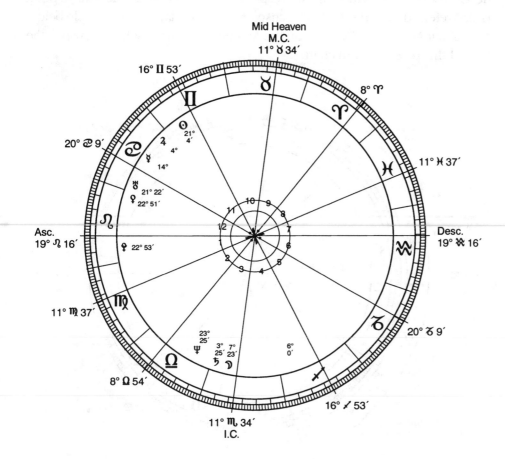

figure 25

House Cusps

The beginning of each house (going counter-clockwise from the Ascendant) is called the cusp of the house. The sign that was on the sunrise point on the horizon determines which sign corresponds to which house. The sunrise point is also referred to as the 1st house cusp or the Ascendant. The example below shows that Aquarius (♒) was on the Ascendant or the first house cusp at the time of this person's birth chart:

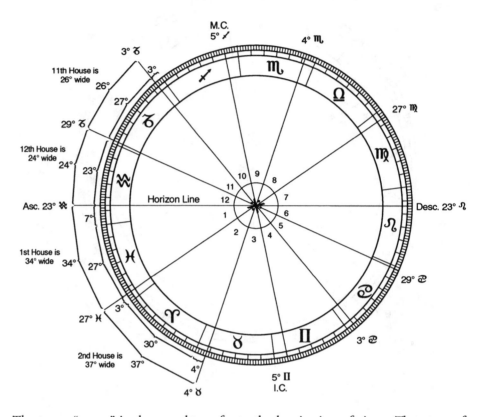

figure 26

The term, "cusp," is also used to refer to the beginning of signs. The cusp of a sign is always 0 degree. The cusp of a house, on the other hand, can line up with any degree of a sign. In the above chart, the first house cusp is 23 degrees Aquarius. The twelfth house cusp happens to fall near the sign cusp between Capricorn and Aquarius since it is lined up on 29 degrees Capricorn.

When a planet is located within five degrees of the next house or sign, you need to consider that the psychological function of the planet is affected by the qualities of both the houses or signs. In Alice's chart her Moon is in the 3rd house, but within 4 degrees of the 4th house, and therefore needs to be considered in relation to both houses.

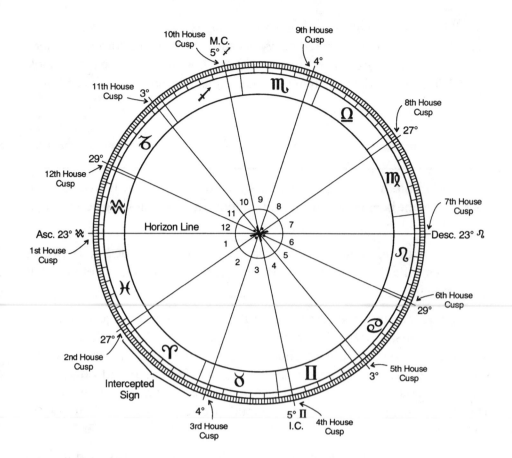

figure 27

Intercepted Signs

By some house division systems, a house will extend such a distance that the next sign following the sign on the house cusp will be totally contained within the boundaries of the house. The sign that is completely within the cusps of a house is called an intercepted sign. In the chart in figure 27, the second and eighth houses contain the intercepted signs of Aries and Libra. Notice that the second and eighth houses are wider than the other houses by a few degrees.

Since the houses containing an intercepted sign are wider, other houses will have to be thinner. In the diagram above notice that the house cusps of both the 5th and 6th line up with Cancer. Also, the cusps of both the 11th and 12th houses line up with Capricorn. Visually you can see that the 5th and 11th houses are thinner, especially when compared to the second and eighth houses.

The sign on the house cusp is said to define an individual's approach to the activities of the house. A person with intercepted signs may often internalize the intercepted signs' psychological qualities and not express these easily. The qualities of an intercepted sign must be blended with the qualities of the sign on the house cusp in which the intercepted sign is contained. In volume two of this workbook series I will provide exercises for you to analyze the signs on the house cusps of your birth chart.

Not all birth chart's will contain intercepted signs. For example, Alice's birth chart does not have intercepted signs, because she was not born in northern latitudes where space appears compressed. It is beyond the scope of this book to explain in more detail why intercepted signs and double signs on house cusps occur.

More about the Relationship between Signs and Houses in Your Birth Chart

The relationship between the cycle of signs and the cycle of houses is often confusing to the beginning astrological student. The two following points might be helpful in clarifying this relationship:

1. Since both signs and houses represent a cycle divided into twelve phases, the corresponding phases have the same developmental meanings.

For example, Aries is the first phase of the cycle of the signs, just as the 1st House is the first phase of the cycle of the house. Both Aries and the 1st house refer to the same developmental qualities. The differences between these two symbolic representations arise in how each manifests in an individual's life. Aries manifests as an inner urge to act in an assertive and initiating manner. The first house manifests as a need to experience activities in life where we can assert ourselves strongly, such as in competitive or physical activities.

2. In a birth chart, the signs and houses that naturally correspond to each other do not generally line up together. The Ascendant, or 1st house cusp, is the beginning of the cycle of houses. The beginning point of the cycle of signs is zero degrees Aries. By determining which sign is on your Ascendant at birth, you are determining how far to shift the zero point of Aries around the cycle of houses. This will then allow the correct sign and degree to line up with the 1st house cusp.

The fact that the two cycles shift according to the exact moment and place of your birth demonstrates how the birth chart symbolizes your own unique individual approach to the rhythms of life.

In summary, the cycle of the seasons (signs) is the basic frame of reference used to determine the positions of the planets, and where each house begins. The exact time and place of birth on earth provide the basic reference point that indicates where the 1st house or Ascendant begins, and which signs line up with which houses.

Most birth chart forms display the houses as equal divisions, mainly for convenience of drawing the chart. The chart in figures 26 and 27 would normally be drawn in the following way:

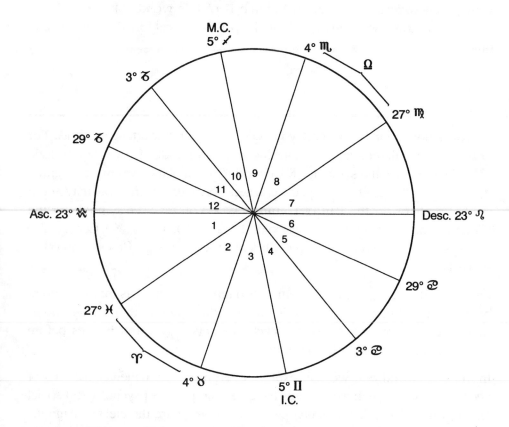

figure 28

In reading the above chart you have to imagine the outer cycle, the cycle of the seasons. In order to determine the lengths of the houses you have to compare the sign degrees of the house cusps.

Take a moment to study Alice's chart on page 7. First find in which house the beginning (0 degrees Aries) of the cycle of the seasons is located. Compare this with the degree of the sign on the Ascendant. Determine the relative lengths of the houses of her birth chart and see if you can find her widest house. Next look at her planets in her birth chart. Notice that her Sun is in Gemini and her Jupiter is in Cancer, but they are both in the 11th house. Notice that her Neptune is in Libra and Saturn is in Scorpio but they are both in the 3rd house.

Planetary Aspects

As the planets revolve in their cycles they continually form complex and meaningful relationships to each other. This workbook focuses on analyzing how signs and house positions help to define the way of acting and focuses of your psychological functions. In Volume II of this workbook series, I will provide you exercises to analyze how the psychological functions affect each other.

Other Important Symbolism

As you study your birth chart you will see other important symbols. For example, you will see symbols for the Moon's North Node (☊) and South Node (☋). You may see the symbol, (℞), denoting that a planet was in a retrograde motion from the earth's perspective when you were born. You may see a symbol perhaps for the Part of Fortune (⊗). You may see symbols for the Planet Chiron (⚷) and for the Asteroids Pallas (⚴), Juno (⚵), Ceres (⚳) and Vesta (⚶). Eventually you will learn the meaning of these and other symbols.

Just like any other complex system of thought, astrology has many different branches and focuses of study. It is important, though, to thoroughly understand the basic symbolism of the cycle, planets, signs, and houses before approaching other astrological symbolism.

In the next workbook we will explore even more fundamental patterns of energy and see how these patterns have meaning to our psychological-social realm of life. These fundamental patterns of energy are the electro-magnetic polarity, the modalities (Cardinal, Fixed, Mutable) and Elements (Fire, Earth, Air, Water). We will see how these patterns also follow cyclical phases of development.

As you explore astrological symbolism, you need to determine its validity in part by how it relates to and derives its meaning from the fundamental pattern of the cycle.

Appendix III
How To Interpret
Astrological Symbolism

This book contains exercises and sentences for you to complete with appropriate keywords and phrases. These sentences, keywords and phrases correspond to the combinations of psychological qualities in your own birth chart. These exercises allow you to translate astrological symbolism and terminology into everyday language.

I have also provided questions and spaces to write your answers to assist you in interpreting what the combinations of psychological qualities could mean to you. The questions on these worksheets correspond to the following in-depth method of interpreting astrological symbolism. These eight steps can be used to increase your awareness of how you can develop and actualize the positive potentials of your individuality.

Steps 1 to 3 will allow you to blend the combination of astrological symbolism in general terms. Then the final 4 steps will allow you to relate the symbolism to yourself.

Before you begin to read the discussion of these steps, I recommend that you choose one of your psychological functions (planets) to analyze. By applying each step, after you read the discussion about it, to one of your psychological functions, you will be able to make the abstract concepts more concrete in your mind.

Creative Blending of this Combination of Astrological Symbols (Steps 1-3)

STEP 1: Determine if this combination of psychological qualities seems compatible? In what ways? Does the combination seem incompatible? In what ways?

Ask yourself whether the way of acting (sign position) or the focus of activity (house position) is compatible with the psychological function (planet) that you are analyzing. If so, define what ways the psychological qualities seem compatible. If the combinations of psychological qualities seem incompatible, define in what ways.

As you learn to interpret the combinations of astrological symbolism in your natal chart, you will always will be assessing various types of compatibilities and incompatibilities represented by blends of psychological qualities. Some psychological qualities flow well with or are supportive of other psychological qualities. There are also some psychological qualities that have conflicts of interests or differences with other psychological qualities. However, astrological principles maintain that *every relationship between psychological qualities can be blended or directed toward positive and constructive expressions or activities.*

Let's look at a few examples:

Mercury in Virgo:

I am inclined to use my rational mind by acting *analytically, with attention to details, discriminatingly, critically.*

The rational mind is inherently compatible with the analytical qualities and natural inclinations of the phase of development that Virgo represents. Even though this combination can also be used negatively (too critically), both psychological qualities represent the same emphasis on the development and use of concrete mental analysis.

Mercury in Pisces:

I am inclined to use my rational mind by acting *empathetically, spiritually, dreamily, moodily, unconsciously, with confusion.*

The rational mind is incompatible with the Piscean inclination to focus on inner, transcendental spiritual realities. The thinking function would tend to become easily confused by the constant flow of emotions and images from the unconscious and/or psychic perceptions.

Venus in the 7th House:

I am inclined to express my social nature by focusing on *one-to-one relationships, creating social harmony, co-operating with others.*

The social developmental inclination of the 7th house is compatible with the psychological function represented by Venus, the part of our psyche that allows us to be mentally receptive to the inclinations and feelings of others.

Venus in the 5th house:

I am inclined to express my social nature by focusing on my *creative self-expression, self-satisfaction* and pleasure, giving and receiving special attention.

The social nature of Venus is both compatible and incompatible with the psychological developmental qualities of fifth house activities, where self-expression is the focus. A fifth house focus may allow a person to be warm and playful with others, but the tendency is for the self to come first before the needs of others.

Venus in the fifth house is not clearly compatible or incompatible. This example represents two important concepts in interpreting astrological symbolism:

1. No combination of psychological qualities is good or bad. Another way of expressing this concept is that all combinations of psychological qualities have both positive and negative potentials.

2. To determine how a combination of psychological qualities might manifest in your life requires you to consider a complex range of factors. Each combination of psychological qualities has to be interpreted within the following contexts:

    a. All the developmental inclinations and potentials of the your psyche (symbolized by your birth chart)

    b. Your environmental conditions (past, present and potential future environmental conditions)

    c. The choices that you have made in your life.

You cannot expect easy rules, clear-cut yes-or-no, do-this-or-do-that answers from astrology. Your birth chart represents your individual potentials on an abstract level. Your psyche will attempt to develop its potentials, and whether you are conscious of your natural inclinations or not, you will exhibit characteristics and focuses emphasized in your birth chart. However, ultimately what you do with your special individual potentials depends on a number of factors, such as how aware you are, how determined you are, as well as the circumstances of your environment.

Astrology offers us a system of understanding how principles that derive from the cyclical development of energy can apply and give order to your everyday life. You have control over whether the environment will totally define your individuality, or whether you will be able to develop your individual potentials in the ways that you want by living in harmony with the cycles of the universe.

As you become more skilled in interpreting astrological symbolism you may skip Step 1, or at least move quickly to the next two steps. But at first, work through this step in order to get yourself used to thinking in terms of compatibilities and incompatibilities of psychological qualities.

I recommend you now turn to one of the psychological functions (planets) that you have chosen to analyze and apply this first step. You may want to make notes in the space provided in the book or on a separate sheet of paper.

STEP 2: Creative Blending Of Positive Potentials

In this step, we will move beyond assessing the compatibility and incompatibility of a combination of psychological qualities. Ask yourself, how can the way of acting and/or life activity enhance the psychological function. Creatively blend the combination of psychological qualities to identify positive potentials for yourself.

Ask yourself "In what positive ways can this combination of psychological qualities be used?"

Allow yourself to come up with new ideas, to "brainstorm" the many different things that a person with this energy blend can do with ease. Try to think of positive ways of acting and/or focuses of activity in life that these combinations of psychological qualities can represent. It may be helpful to picture a person other than yourself — imaginary or real — who uses these characteristics and focuses in ideal, positive ways.

At this point it is important that you do not limit your thinking by only considering how this energy blend might just relate to you. Temporarily exclude your personal focus on whether any of these behaviors, activities or experiences that you list are describing you. In steps 4-8 you will come back to these positive and negative potentials that you identified and determine which relate to you, and which potentials on your list might be new life directions to focus on and develop within yourself.

Let's return to two of the examples that we used in the previous step to illustrate how to creatively blend positive potentials.

Mercury in Virgo

Creative blending of positive potentials: The rational mind is enhanced by the analytical developmental potentials of Virgo. The mind can be used to analyze data and information. A tendency to focus on details would make a career involving research a positive potential. The individual might use this inclination for technical thinking in careers of medicine, business, law, and even artistic pursuits such as film making where lab work and editing are necessary. Other inclinations of the psyche, symbolized by the whole birth chart, would determine where and how this analytical psychological function would be used. The individual would have the potential for establishing maintenance routines to ensure physical health as well as a neat, well-kept physical environment. Gardening might be a meaningful pursuit. In relationships, he or she would look for ways to be helpful to others. This individual would not demand the center of attention but would be willing to jump in and do what's necessary to make things go right.

Mercury in Pisces

The rational mind could be used in artistic, creative, imaginative pursuits such as singing or playing music, writing poetry, painting. The mind could also be used to communicate in everyday terms those emotional perceptions from higher, universal spiritual realities or those psychological, unconscious realities. An individual with this placement could be an artist, a counselor or a psychologist. The important thing about this combination of psychological qualities is that the individual is required to value the rational mind and see the importance of developing the logical, everyday intellect in order to fully make use of the highly refined emotional perceptions that she or he feels and receives.

In order to creatively blend, or "brainstorm" as complete a list of possibilities or potentials as you can, the following suggestions might be helpful to stimulate, as well as focus, your imagination and thinking.

"Brainstorm" General Psychological Characteristics

First combine the psychological characteristics of the different symbolism into general psychological descriptions. Combine the keywords of the different symbols to describe general behavior and focuses in life. Remember that you are not trying to describe yourself particularly in this step.

Relate Symbolism to Specific Areas of Life

Then begin to think of specific ways of being, activities and life directions. What activities, pastimes or behavior would a person with these general psychological qualities find natural to do, or be drawn to do? You might find it helpful to keep in mind the following different areas of life as you creatively blend qualities symbolized in your birth chart:

Career-Community Service: Activities or ways of being that give a reputation in the community, and allow you to meet community responsibilities.

Income: Activities or ways of being that get paid for, and that help meet survival needs.

Personal Fulfillment: Activities or ways of being that may not be monetarily satisfying, but are personally satisfying.

Leisure: Activities or ways of being that are relaxing, pleasurable and playful.

Relationships: Activities or ways of being that are useful in positive social interaction.

Artistic Expression: Activities or ways of being that suggest particular creative artistic expression.

Health: Activities or ways of being that would be useful to your physical and emotional well-being.

Spiritual: Activities or ways of being that are useful in transcendental, spiritual development.

As you apply your creative blending to these areas, remember that some activities, or ways of being, may overlap and relate to more than one category. Also, some psychological characteristic may not apply to all of these areas. There are activities, or ways of being, which a person gets paid for that may not be self-fulfilling or satisfying; similarly there are other activities, or ways of being, that are self-fulfilling for which an individual may never receive payment nor community recognition.

Example from Alice's Birth Chart

The following creative blending of Alice's Moon in Scorpio in the third house illustrates this second step of interpreting this combination of psychological qualities and positive potentials.

"Brainstorm" General Psychological Characteristics

An in-depth emotional (Scorpio) response (Moon) to day-to-day life and to her style of thinking (3rd house). Penetrating (Scorpio) emotional nature (Moon) could be used in mental, communicative activities (3rd house). Speaking and communicating ability can deeply affect others. Could probe into and respond to the deep emotional states of others in learning and communicating experiences. She would be drawn to magnetic creative learning and teaching experiences. She would feel the urge to use the rational mind (3rd house) to probe into the psychological states of others, or into mysteries or information that might be hidden or kept secret (Scorpio). Emotional control emphasized.

Symbolism Related to Specific Areas of Life

Money and Income: Counseling, teaching, research, writing, collecting data that involves in-depth interpersonal probing, emotional healing linked to rational mind (doctor, nursing.) Investigative pursuits in reporting, police or private detective work.

Personal Fulfillment: Learning and teaching information with others can be emotionally satisfying. Experiences that involve emotional discipline in order to creatively direct mental and physical dexterity can be emotionally satisfying. (Playing musical instruments, physical activities such as dance, running and gymnastics). Intense interpersonal emotional sharing and sexuality are important. Psychological growth experiences through self-education.

Leisure: Reading books that probe deeply into psychological natures of individuals. Reading mystery stories. Writing journals. Relating to an intimate partner in an intense emotional and sexual manner could be a preferred pleasurable activity.

Relationships: Ability to communicate with others on a deep emotional level. Magnetism in interpersonal relationships. Peak experiences through sexual expression and union. Ability to respond to others with intensity adding depth to relationships.

Artistic Expression: Artistic expression that requires depth of emotional expression, and mental or physical dexterity. Art expression must deeply affect others. Emotional concentration allows discipline in creative expression.

Health: Emotional control leading to discipline in avoiding aspects of life that are unhealthy. The ability to transform and release blocked and repressed emotions helps to maintain a healthy state.

Spirituality: Emotional concentration can allowing for the elevation of her overly selfish emotions, and the ability to master spiritual disciplines.

Sometimes it is difficult to think of new life directions because we have unconsciously become rigid and conditioned to thinking within a narrow perspective. These first two-steps are aimed at helping you get past self-limiting perspectives in order to objectively generate a list of new possibilities. The more choices a person can see and act upon, the richer life can be.

I recommend you now turn to the psychological function that you are analyzing and apply this second step. You may want to write notes in the space provided in the book or on a separate sheet of paper.

STEP 3: Creative Blending Of Negative Potentials

As you blended the psychological qualities in step one, you may have also thought of some negative potentials the symbolism could represent. The advantage of thinking of the positive potentials first is that it can train you to see what can be in terms of positive growth potential. However, we also have to be aware of the negative potentials for possible tensions, conflicts, self-defeating behavior, incompatibilities, inhibitions and extremism in our personalities and lives.

It is important to understand the nature of negative potentials within your psyche. Negative psychological characteristics can result from two main sources: too much tension and too much ease.

Tension – Blends of Psychological Qualities That Are Too Different

When opposing psychological qualities are related to each other by their position in the chart, a potential for incompatibility and tension exists. This tension can indicate possible conflicts within the psyche. Extremism or inhibitions can result if one quality dominates the other.

Example:

Alice's Mars in Capricorn offers a good example of this type of tension.

Negative potentials: Her capacity for spontaneity could be inhibited by an inclination for self-control and sense of responsibility. Sexual inhibition and guilt can result. Willpower could be misused in aggressively pursuing overly ambitious goals.

Ease – Blends of Psychological Qualities that are Too Much Alike

It is possible for psychological qualities within a psyche to be so flowing and compatible that the individual does not notice them, and therefore does not develop these qualities to their fullest potential. On the other hand, if a psychological function is blended with the exact same energy quality in its sign or house position a certain psychological energy quality could be developed to a negative extreme.

Example:

Alice's chart does not contain a planet in its natural sign. I will use Mars in its natural sign, Aries, to illustrate this point so that you can make a comparison between the two sign placements of this planet.

The potentials for the negative psychological qualities to be manifested could be heightened since Mars might be unchecked in its expression. This blend of psychological qualities could manifest in a negative manner as overbearing, aggressive, impulsive, rash psychological tendencies.

To overcome differences and conflicts of interest within yourself requires the development of strength of character and purpose.

Our challenge is to find how two different qualities can work together in a positive manner. Tensions and incompatibilities can stimulate an individual to be more conscious of both of the psychological qualities in a particular combination. Capricorn, for instance, can give Mars' impulsive energy a sense of regulation and sustained direction, while Mars can add initiative and innovation to the constructive characteristics of Capricorn.

Similar psychological qualities represent a potential flow in functioning that can easily be translated into talent if you consciously develop it. Mars in Aries suggests a potential for tremendous energy and willpower if it is consciously and positively directed and balanced with other sides of the psyche.

In this third step, therefore, explore the potential for behavioral problems that a significant combination of psychological qualities might represent. Think of negative ways a particular blend of psychological qualities could manifest in anyone. Again, at this point it may be helpful to be unconcerned about whether or not these negative potentials relate to you. Be detached and objective.

Negative potentials of Alice's Moon in Scorpio in the Third House:

Let's return to Alice's Moon in Scorpio in the third house to illustrate Step 3 of this interpretive process.

Difficulties in expressing herself as her personal emotional nature could be repressed and held inside by Scorpio urges. Intense emotional feelings could cloud rational focus. Emotional intensity and control could inhibit the third house inclination for change and mental flexibility. Could be too emotionally demanding on herself and others in learning and teaching situations. Could be possessive and revengeful.

By working with these feelings in her psychological nature, she could learn to recognize and deal with her deep intense inclinations for emotional sharing and expression. She is challenged to develop many creative physical, and mental outlets in order to express and release her powerful emotions. She is also challenged to work at developing mental objectivity.

I recommend you now return to the psychological function that you are analyzing and apply this third step. You may want to make notes the space provided in the book or on a separate sheet of paper.

STEP 4: Identify the positive potentials of this blend of psychological qualities that you recognize exist in your psychological nature now

What expressions, experiences or situations of your life relate to the blend of psychological qualities that you are analyzing? It is important for you to determine how you are (and have been) developing the potentials symbolized by this blend of psychological qualities before you can determine what new directions and alternatives will be appropriate for you. To fully answer these questions you might need to look carefully and objectively at all stages of your life, including early childhood.

This step might be the easiest part of this in-depth interpretative process. The first three steps were aimed at helping you see beyond your subjective view of yourself. With this fourth step, you will be able to objectively see how the energy blends of your birth chart relate to you personally.

Ultimately, one of the most important skills that astrology can teach you is the ability to be objective about yourself. Working with the symbolism of your astrological birth chart gives you a mirror that allows you to see yourself more clearly, to see past your blind spots, and to see yourself honestly without personal, subjective distortions. Of course, you might still see only what you want to see about yourself. But this eight-step process can give you an opportunity to develop your sense of personal objectivity.

Example:

Alice's Moon in Scorpio in the Third House

On pages 109-114 we have seen that using her rational mind, learning as well as relationships are important concerns and focuses for Alice. She started playing the piano at age six, an activity which requires mental and physical dexterity (Third House). She has also continued studying and playing the piano through childhood and into early adulthood, which suggests an ability to be emotionally disciplined (Scorpio). These are some ways this blend of psychological qualities relates to her life.

I recommend you now return to the psychological function that you are analyzing and apply this fourth step. You may want to make notes in the space provided in the book or on a separate sheet of paper.

STEP 5: Determine which of these existing positive potentials you want to improve and develop further or use in new ways. Define in what new ways.

Each individual continues to grow and develop throughout his/her life. Attributes or skills can always be developed further and used in new positive ways. It is not enough to have been compassionate or responsible, or artistically skillful in playing the piano during a certain phase of life. We must continue to develop our psychological functions, ways of acting, and focuses of activities throughout our lives and apply them in new expressions and activities.

Example.

Alice's Moon in Scorpio in 3rd house:

Alice might want to continue to develop her ability to play the piano for performances or for teaching, or perhaps to eventually compose music. She may use her psychological function for deep insight in another area such as counseling. She may decide she wants to more positively develop how she uses this function in emotionally sharing with her friends and her intimate partner.

I recommend you now return to the psychological function that you are analyzing and apply this fifth step. You may want to make notes in the space provided in the book or on a separate sheet of paper.

STEP 6: Choose new positive potentials of this combination of psychological qualities that you want to actualize

Recognizing new possibilities for yourself is an exciting and renewing experience. Some people see too few new alternatives and possibilities for themselves. If you have been able to complete STEP 2 satisfactorily, you will not have this problem. Other people see too many possibilities and alternatives, and cannot decide which new options are truly in tune with their individual natures. These last steps require that you develop the ability to make decisions and choices. The more you work with your birth chart, the more you will be able to tune into the full range of potentials that exist within you.

The following suggestion might be useful to help you focus on specific new life directions that you would like to explore, or new ways of being that you would like to develop. Look over the list of positive potentials that you made in STEP 2, and get in touch with what you spontaneously and emotionally feel drawn to, regardless of practical concerns. Do not limit yourself by thinking of all the reasons you cannot do something you may feel drawn to. Give yourself permission to see yourself in new ways. Getting in touch with what you want to do is the first step towards making new potentials a reality in your life.

Example.

In assessing her Moon in Scorpio in the 3rd house, Alice could decide that she wants to use her potentials to probe deep within (Scorpio) her own personal emotional inclinations (Moon) in order to write (3rd house) about her psychological growth (Moon in Scorpio).

I recommend you now return to the psychological function that you are analyzing and apply this sixth step. You may want to make notes in the space provided in the book or on a separate sheet of paper.

STEP 7: Identify negative behavior patterns associated with this combination of psychological qualities you want to overcome

How do you overcome negative behavior patterns associated with a planet/sign or planet /house combination? To start you must fully accept both of the psychological qualities of the combination. For example, an individual who has Mercury in Pisces has two psychological qualities so different from each other that the psyche may have had to unconsciously choose one over the other. With this combination the individual may become obsessed with developing the rational mind and ignore or even discount inner, emotional needs and inclinations. Conversely, the individual may become a "space case," existing in a dream world without being able to think or communicate logically. Of course most people will not become either extreme, but the point is, negative behavior or patterns can develop when the individual is discounting or ignoring one side of self.

By accepting both of the psychological qualities that are involved in the negative behavior, you can begin to focus on developing the quality that has been discounted. In the example of Mercury in Pisces, the individual may want to develop his/her rational thinking process more or may want to find ways of being more open to his or her inner world of dreams and emotional perceptions.

Example:

Alice's Moon in Scorpio in 3rd House

Alice could use journal writing (3rd house) as a method of psychological catharsis and transformation (Scorpio) to overcome her personal insecurities and fears (Moon).

I recommend you now return to the psychological function that you are analyzing and apply this seventh step. You may want to make notes in the space provided in the book or on a separate sheet of paper.

STEP 8: Goal setting: determine specific actions and timelines (short-term, long-term goals) for developing the positive potentials of this combination of psychological qualities.

This step is aimed at keeping this interpretative process from just being an intellectual pursuit. In order for you to actualize your potentials, you must make the transition from being conscious of a potential for action to taking necessary actions.

What Can You Do Now

Determine which of the positive potentials to which you feel drawn could be added to your life without a great deal of preparation – without a great deal of expenditure of money, or without a great deal of time spent in training, or without having to free yourself from complicated ties and responsibilities.

Most new sides of self can be developed and experienced in your daily life on a personal level. Sometimes what starts out as leisure and self-fulfillment pursuits can turn into activities that lead to a career.

Example:

Alice's Moon in Scorpio in the third house could imply potential for a counseling career (the ability to respond to others (Moon) in deep emotionally transforming ways (Scorpio) in experiences that help to make mental connections and allow you to communicate ideas (third house). Even if a counseling career seems impractical or a long way off, Alice could still be exploring the subject by reading (third house) books about counseling. She could seek opportunities in which she herself goes through counseling experiences. She might be a "natural counselor" with her friends by helping them get in touch with and talk about their deep emotions and feelings (third house Scorpio).

We often avoid doing new things because we feel we have to be perfect, or have to meet up to high standards (usually set by someone else). One way to rise above this is to realize that perfection is only an illusion, and that the process rather than the end result is a more important focus. If we have handled the process well, the end result will be meaningful and satisfying, whether or not it measures up to the expectations of others, or even when the product is not what we imagined it would be.

Long Range Objectives and Planning

Consider new directions and ways of being that do require in-depth preparation, training or a major re-ordering of your life. The development of new potentials and alternative life directions will require patience and sustained effort over a long period of time. Awareness of your major life cycles and rhythms would be helpful. You may find it beneficial to consult an astrologer and/or counselor to aid in your decision-making, goal-setting and planning.

I recommend you now return to the psychological function that you are analyzing and apply this eighth step. You may want to make notes in the space provided(the last page of the planet's section) or on a separate sheet of paper.

Summary

Following these eight steps will allow you to use the exercises of this workbook to generate new directions for your life. These directions will be based on your inner inclinations and potentials as symbolized by your birth chart.

Understanding yourself and your potentials astrologically requires that you use your imagination (Neptune), your mental intuitiveness (Uranus), as well as the analytical, rational faculties of your mind (Mercury). You have to be mentally open (Uranus) to the positive possibilities of what each planet, sign and house combination could mean (Jupiter)to you. To gain this understanding requires that you creatively synthesize or blend (Mercury and Jupiter) various, sometimes contradictory psychological qualities. Part of this creativity is the ability to accept ambiguity and to work with the many possibilities any particular combination of symbols can represent. You will need patience and the ability to sustain your efforts (Saturn). You will also need to be able to act (Mars) upon your understandings, and to know when you have to rely on others (Venus and Pluto).

It is through this process of creatively blending different psychological qualities of yourself that you can move toward being a more whole, balanced, self-actualized individual able to freely and consciously choose the directions your life will take.

In summary, the eight steps for an in-depth interpretation of significant combinations of your astrological symbolism are listed below:

STEP 1: Determine if the combination of psychological qualities seems compatible? In what ways? Determine if the combination seems incompatible? In what ways?

STEP 2: Creative blending of the positive potentials of this combination of psychological qualities.

STEP 3. Creative blending of the negative potentials of this combination of psychological qualities.

Creative Blending Of This Combination Of Astrological Symbols

---

STEP 4: Identify the positive potentials of this blend of psychological qualities you recognize now exist in your psychological nature.

STEP 5: Determine which of these existing positive potentials you want to develop further or use in new ways. Define in what new ways.

STEP 6: Choose new positive potentials of this combination of psychological qualities you want to actualize.

STEP 7: Identify negative behavior patterns associated with this combination of psychological qualities you want to overcome.

STEP 8: Goal setting: determine specific actions and timelines (short-term, long-term goals) for developing the positive potentials of this combination of psychological qualities.

Relating This Combination Of Astrological Symbols To Yourself

Appendix IV: Creative Blending Of The Sign and House Positions Of The Planets in Alice's Birth Chart

Personal Background

When Alice became an astrology student of mine in 1978 at age 24, she had a number of questions which she was trying to answer for herself. These questions concerned basic issues of life: self-image, personal satisfaction, relationships, career choices.

Alice, a university student, had been trying to choose one from several career directions. When she began studying at the university at age 18, she chose courses in history, anthropology and urban planning. At age 21, she was drawn to study medicine, and at age 21, began taking courses in biology and chemistry. She was fascinated by these subjects, even though the learning of highly technical and scientific information did not come easy to her. She continued to struggle with the courses, because of her interest in medicine and because she felt that she should be able to learn the material.

All during this time Alice was studying music. She had been playing the piano since age six, and had studied all types of music from classical to jazz. However, though a talented and accomplished musician, she did not feel comfortable or confident with the idea of performing before an audience. She felt a dilemma between her inclination to focus attention on her own self-expression and her inclination to contribute to society in some way. She gave private piano lessons to children and adults to make extra money.

Alice was also trying to sort out her relationship needs. She was involved in an intimate relationship which had both excitement and tension. She felt the person with whom she was involved was warm, charming and adventurous, but not consistent. When Alice came to me, this particular relationship was in the process of ending.

Relationships in general were another concern for Alice. She tended to be overly sensitive in social situations. She said she could tell when others became emotionally uncomfortable and it affected her deeply. She constantly wanted to take care of others and make them feel safe and secure. She also felt others had emotional "hidden agendas," and if these deep feelings were not being expressed, she would feel "anxious and confused." She said she felt she needed people too much, and she was not able to detach herself from others who were affecting her in a negative manner.

Alice decided in the mid-1980's to begin a two-year Video Production Program at a local community college. After completing this program she spent the next 5 years producing videos for local corporations. She worked in the production department of a local television station.

Recently, Alice quit her job at the television station and applied for a position in the Peace Corps. She felt a need to experience what it was like to give direct service to people, preferably in a multi-cultural setting.

Creative Blending Of Alice's Planets In Their Signs And House Positions

The following pages include creative blendings of the signs and house positions of the planets in Alice's birth chart. For the purposes of this book these creative blendings have been written in a shortened form, but you will still be able to identify the important repeated themes of Alice's individuality. You will note that some of the symbolism have been more extensively blended than others. As you work with your own birth chart, you will also find that certain combinations of symbolism are more easily blended than others. The type of chart analysis presented in this book is meant to be an on-going process. It will allow you to see new potentials and understand more about yourself at each new phase of life.

Sun in Gemini in the Eleventh House

Blending of Positive Potentials: Individual life purpose (Sun) would be centered on a rational approach (Gemini) to symbolic thinking (llth house). This approach could be used in inventing new ideas based upon existing systems of thought. Music, math, computer science, astrology, linguistics would be examples of symbolic languages which could be studied, learned, communicated to others. Sun in Gemini in the 11th house represents that Alice's individuality is naturally inclined toward using her mind to focus on inventive, technical creativity. This Gemini position of her Sun can also represent a curiosity about world cultures, while the eleventh house position can represent an inclination to be socially concerned about the well-being of all peoples of the world.

Blending of Negative Potentials: If Alice's rational, logical way of acting (Gemini) is over developed, it could block her involvement in activities that would allow her to develop her intuitive, inventive mental abilities (11th house). If her rational, logical way of acting is not fully developed, activities that involve mental inventiveness and higher thinking might reflect an unpredictability and eccentricity.

Moon in Scorpio in the Third House, close to the Fourth House

Blending of Positive Potentials: A potential exists for Alice to have an intense, in-depth (Scorpio) emotional response (Moon) to her everyday personal environment (3rd house). Penetrating (Scorpio) emotional nature (Moon) could be used in mental, communicative activities (3rd house), such as counseling, research, writing. A potential exists to use communicative activities (3rd house) to probe deeply into emotional, psychological states of others (Scorpio), especially those emotional states relating to personal feelings of insecurity (4th house, Moon). Magnetic (Scorpio) and responsive (Moon) approach to teaching (3rd house). Intense relationships (Scorpio) and feelings of well-being (Moon) based upon educational experiences (3rd house). She might have a tendency to base her emotional securities (Moon close to the 4th house) on intimate relationships (Scorpio). Activities related to her personal stability and feelings of security (Moon and 4th house) could go through many transformations as a result of deep emotional sharing in relationships (Scorpio).

Blending of Negative Potentials: Intense emotional feelings (Moon, Scorpio) could interfere with activities requiring clear rational focus (3rd house). Personal emotions and feelings (Moon) could be repressed and held inside by Scorpio tendencies. Emotional intensity and control (Scorpio) could inhibit her potential for change and mental flexibility (3rd house).

Mercury in Cancer in Eleventh House, close to the Twelfth House

Blending of Positive Potentials: Alice has a potential to think (Mercury) of ways that society could nurture all individuals (11th house) and give them emotional security (Cancer). She has a potential to gather information and study (Mercury) common cultural traditions (Cancer) of different peoples of the world (11th house) — an interest in anthropological, multi-cultural studies, providing assistance to people in developing countries. Rational synthesis (Mercury) of creative, symbolic ideas in ways that would express personal emotions (Cancer) — musical improvisation, creative writing, photography, etc. Use of mass media (11th house) to communicate (Mercury) personal feelings (Cancer). A potential to study (Mercury) the collective unconscious or spiritual pursuits (twelfth house) in order to gain personal, emotional clarity (Cancer). A potential to communicate (Mercury) in a personal manner (Cancer) to people from different cultures and backgrounds (11th House), as well as refined feelings of universal beauty and harmony (12th house). A potential to communicate (Mercury) to others in highly emotional ways (Cancer, 12th house).

Blending of Negative Potentials: Her subjective emotions (Cancer) could confuse her rational thinking process (Mercury). Could be difficult to develop rational objectivity (Mercury) with such inner focus (Cancer, 12th house).

Venus in Cancer in the Twelfth House

Blending of Positive Potentials: There could be an attraction (Venus) to traditional, classical (Cancer) expressions of art. An emotional inclination (Cancer) to be receptive (Venus) to inner needs of others, to give in ways that would nurture others' feelings of well-being (Venus in Cancer in 12th house). These qualities could be used in counseling, or in a "mother" role, either personally or in a large-scale human service situation (12th House).

Blending of Negative Potentials: Personal insecurities and defenses (Cancer) could inhibit her social nature (Venus). Her social nature (Venus) is turned inward (12th house) and could be withdrawn and/or taken advantage of by other people's difficulties or weaknesses (12th house). Receptivity to others could be clouded by her emotional inclinations (Cancer, 12th house).

Mars in Capricorn in the Fifth House

Blending of Positive Potentials: Alice's constructive (Capricorn) personal drives (Mars) are focused on creative, artistic activities (5th house). Her physical activity (Mars) tends to be focused on highly structured (Capricorn) recreational games and activities(5th house). Her energy (Mars) is capable of great physical endurance and sustained efforts (Capricorn) and can be used in such sports activities (5th house) as long-distance running. Her personal energy (Mars) is enhanced by effective organization and her inclination for achievement (Capricorn). She has a capacity to start (Mars) creative projects (5th house) that have realistic goals for completion (Capricorn).

Blending of Negative Potentials: Alice's urges for responsibility and the setting of limits (Capricorn) could restrict and inhibit her spontaneity (Mars) and/or creative expressions (5th house). It might be difficult for her to be spontaneous in playful and leisure activities (5th house) because something always has to be done (Capricorn).

Jupiter in Cancer in the Eleventh House

Blending of Positive Potentials: Alice has a potential to abstractly understand and translate (Jupiter) highly symbolic language (llth house) into personal feelings (Cancer). She has a potential to develop belief systems (Jupiter) based on a personal (Cancer), holistic (llth house) approach to the world. Her creative expansion (Jupiter) is based on a personal approach (Cancer) to symbolic thinking (llth house) with a reference to the past (Cancer). She could involve herself in activities using mass media (llth house) to teach other people (Jupiter) methods of developing personal acceptance and positive feelings about self (Cancer). She is a seeking truth and knowledge (Jupiter) in the personal traditions (Cancer) of all cultures of the world (llth house), which relates to her interest in anthropology. She could have idealistic beliefs (Jupiter) that everyone in the world (llth house) should have the necessary living comforts (Cancer). She has the potential to administrate (Jupiter) organizations directed toward humanitarian goals, such as hospitals or perhaps an international (11th house) hostel (Cancer) for world-wide travelers (Jupiter). She could be a proprietress (Jupiter) of a cosmopolitan (11th house) restaurant (Cancer).

Blending of Negative Potentials: Alice's subjective, personal emotional inclination (Cancer) could cloud her objective, abstract mind. Her personal emotional defensiveness (Cancer) could keep her continually searching (Jupiter) for ideal groups to relate to (11th house), never allowing her to be satisfied. This same pattern could give her a tendency to be drawn to eccentric, even rebellious activities.

Saturn in Scorpio in the Third House

Blending of Positive Potentials: The discipline of Saturn and emotional control of Scorpio would give tremendous concentration and depth in thinking and learning situations (3rd house). Structured, ordered. realistic self-education. Education is seen mainly as a means to achieve a position in society. The potential exists for very practical and mature applications of education (3rd house) that would help others grow psychologically (Scorpio).

Intense, psychological transformations and changes (Scorpio) could occur in her sense of emotional security and well-being (4th house), as she meets difficult tests and challenges (Saturn). Developing patience and perseverance (Saturn) will help her cope emotionally with life (Scorpio, 4th house). Personal, emotional security (4th house) is enhanced by commitment and order (Saturn) of an intimate relationship (Scorpio). She would have the potential and inclination to establish enduring (Saturn) personal relationships (Scorpio).

Blending of Negative Potentials: Saturn in the third house could symbolize self-doubt and insecurities about one's mental, rational learning ability. Could avoid completing or even entering into learning activities for fear of being judged too harshly. Saturn close to the fourth house in Scorpio could imply emotional (4th house) self-doubt (Saturn), especially in interpersonal relationships (Scorpio), because of feelings that she is being judged (Saturn). She might feel insecure about being rejected by those with whom she becomes emotionally close.

Uranus in Cancer in the Twelfth House

Blending of Positive Potentials: She has a potential to use symbolic thinking and communicating (Uranus) to express universal feelings and realities (12th house) in a highly personal, individualistic manner (Cancer); for example, composing music, taking photographs and producing videos — using the inventive, technical mind (Uranus) to capture images (12th house, Cancer) that have personal (Cancer) and universal (12th house) emotional meaning. Her capacity to break away (Uranus) from early childhood conditional habit patterns (Cancer) could be assisted by activities and experiences that would open herself up to spiritual, transcendental realms (12th house). Alice has the potential for emotional (Cancer) independence (Uranus). She has a personal approach (Cancer) to using her inventive, intuitive mind (Uranus) to explore and experience transcendental realms (12th house). She has a potential to communicate to large numbers of people (Uranus) her personal feelings (Cancer) about universal realities (12th house).

Blending of Negative Potentials: Her personal insecurities (Cancer) could block her capacity for progressive, futuristic ideas. The twelfth house position of her Uranus could mean that she would be unconscious of her inclinations for change and breaking outdated emotional habits and patterns; therefore she could be emotionally unpredictable.

Neptune in Libra in the Third House

Blending of Positive Potentials: Alice has an aesthetic and harmonious (Libra) receptivity to inner images. Her refined feelings (Neptune) enhance personal thinking and communication activities (3rd house). She has a highly graceful and refined (Neptune in Libra) approach to communications (3rd house). This potential could be used in music and other artwork, as well as one-to-one counseling and interpersonal relationships (Libra). She has a potential to be sensitive (Neptune) to the ideas and thoughts (3rd house) that are beneath the surface (Neptune) of others (Libra). She has the potential to be an empathetic listener and teacher. If she develops the potentials of this combination of qualities she could assist in situations where differing ideas and perspectives are required to be mediated and compromises found. She has the potential to write poetry and/or spiritual thoughts.

Blending of Negative Potentials: Alice's emotional flow of feelings and urges from her unconscious (Neptune) could cloud her awareness to the needs of others (Libra) and could keep her from effectively participating in activities where the use of her rational mind is required (3rd house).

Pluto in Leo in the First House

Creative Blending of Positive Potentials: Alice has a potential to add emotional depth and purpose (Pluto) to the personal projections (1st house) of her creativity (Leo). She has a potential to deeply move and affect others (Pluto) with her creative expression (Leo). This added intensity, magnetism, and charisma of her personal expression would aid in performing (Leo). Pluto in Leo in the 1st house would give her a potential to set in motion a cathartic process of psychological changes in her life, as well as the lives of others through creative expressions. These qualities would be useful in counseling, art, politics, etc.

Blending of Negative Potentials: Pluto's inclination for internal emotional transformation could inhibit her involvement in activities where she would project herself (1st house) in an self-expressive, creative manner (Leo). Pluto's inclination to elevate her selfish drives (Pluto) could inhibit Alice's potential to act on her own behalf when required (1st house), and could inhibit potential to be dramatic and self-expressive or to perform (Leo).

Summary of Repeated Themes of the Planets in Signs and Houses

Venus and Uranus in Cancer in the 11th house: would indicate an inclination to communicate her personal artistic expressions on a mass scale.

Sun in Gemini in the 11th house, Mercury in Cancer in the 11th house: would indicate rational approaches to symbolic thinking — music, astrology, also, humanitarian concerns, especially of a personal nurturing nature.

The Scorpio emphasis and Pluto in the first house, along with Cancer: would indicate an inclination to seek close, intense, interpersonal relationships.

Moon in Scorpio, Pluto in the first house: would indicate an inclination for deep psychological exploration and transformation.

Leo rising, Pluto in the lst house: would indicate a potential to be a creative and/or performing artist with powerful magnetism and charisma.

Mercury in Cancer, Moon in 3rd house: would indicate the use of mental sides of self to draw from and communicate the emotional sides of life.

Appendix V
Additional Sentences For
The Signs And House
Positions Of The Planets
In Your Birth Chart

Additional Sentences For Your Sun Sign

I am inclined to express my individuality in a way that will develop

_____

(developmental potentials)

therefore:

I am inclined to express my individuality by acting

_____

(keywords for sign)

I am inclined to be self-expressive and creative in a way that will develop

_____

(developmental potentials)

therefore:

I am inclined to be self-expressive and creative by acting

_____

(keywords for sign)

I am inclined to express my unique vitality way that will develop

_____

(developmental potentials)

therefore:

I am inclined to express my unique vitality by acting

_____

(keywords for sign)

Additional Sentences
For Your Sun House Position

I am inclined to express my individuality by focusing on activities that will develop

_____

(developmental potentials)

therefore:

I am inclined to express my individuality by focusing on

_____

(keywords for house)

I am inclined to be self-expressive and creative by focusing on activities that will develop

_____

(developmental potentials)

therefore:

I am inclined to be self-expressive and creative by focusing on

_____

(keywords for house)

I am inclined to express my unique vitality by focusing on activities that will develop

_____

(developmental potentials)

therefore:

I am inclined to express my unique vitality by focusing on

_____

(keywords for house)

Additional Sentences For Your Moon Sign

I am inclined to emotionally respond to life in a way that will develop

_____

(developmental potentials)

therefore:

I am inclined to emotionally respond to life by acting

_____

(keywords for sign)

I am inclined to feel a sense of emotional security and well-being in a way that will develop

_____

(developmental potentials)

therefore:

I am inclined to feel a sense of emotionally security and well-being by acting

_____

(keywords for sign)

I am inclined to express my emotional nature in ways that will develop

_____

(developmental potentials)

therefore:

I am inclined to express my emotional nature by acting

_____

(keywords for sign)

Additional Sentences
For Your Moon House Position

I am inclined to emotionally respond to life by focusing on activities that will develop

_____

(developmental potentials)

therefore:

I am inclined to emotionally respond to life by focusing on

_____

(keywords for house)

I am inclined to feel a sense of emotional security and well-being by focusing on activities that will develop

_____

(developmental potentials)

therefore:

I am inclined to be feel a sense of emotional security and well-being by focusing on

_____

(keywords for house)

I am inclined to express my emotional nature by focusing on activities that will develop

_____

(developmental potentials)

therefore:

I am inclined to express my emotional nature by focusing on

_____

(keywords for house)

Additional Sentences For Your Mercury Sign

I am inclined to communicate with others in a way that will develop

_____

(developmental potentials)

therefore:

I am inclined to communicate with others by acting

_____

(keywords for sign)

I am inclined to examine and analyze information in a way that will develop

_____

(developmental potentials)

therefore:

I am inclined to examine and analyze information by acting

_____

(keywords for sign)

I am inclined to use my logical, rational mind in a way that will develop

_____

(developmental potentials)

therefore:

I am inclined to use my logical, rational mind by acting

_____

(keywords for sign)

Additional Sentences For Your Mercury House Position

I am inclined to communicate with others by focusing on activities that will develop

_____

(developmental potentials)

therefore:

I am inclined to communicate with others by focusing on

_____

(keywords for house)

I am inclined to examine and analyze information by focusing on activities that will develop

_____

(developmental potentials)

therefore:

I am inclined to examine and analyze information by focusing on

_____

(keywords for house)

I am inclined to use my rational, logical mind by focusing on activities that will develop

_____

(developmental potentials)

therefore:

I am inclined to use my rational, logical mind by focusing on

_____

(keywords for house)

Additional Sentences For Your Venus Sign

I am inclined to express my likes, dislikes and values in a way that will develop

_____

(developmental potentials)

therefore:

I am inclined to express my likes, dislikes and values by acting

_____

(keywords for sign)

I am inclined to satisfy my sensual and physical needs in a way that will develop

_____

(developmental potentials)

therefore:

I am inclined to express my sensual and physical needs by acting

_____

(keywords for sign)

I am inclined to express my social nature in a way that will develop

_____

(developmental potentials)

therefore:

I am inclined to express my social nature by acting

_____

(keywords for sign)

Additional Sentences
For Your Venus House Position

I am inclined to express my likes, dislikes and values by focusing on activities that will develop

_____

(developmental potentials)

therefore:

I am inclined to express my likes, dislikes and values by focusing on

_____

(keywords for house)

I am inclined to satisfy my sensual and physical needs by focusing on activities that will develop

_____

(developmental potentials)

therefore:

I am inclined to express my sensual and physical needs by focusing on

_____

(keywords for house)

I am inclined to express my social nature by focusing on activities that will develop

_____

(developmental potentials)

therefore:

I am inclined to express my social nature by focusing on

_____

(keywords for house)

Additional Sentences For Your Mars Sign

I am inclined to express my sexual drives and desires in a way that will develop

_____

(developmental potentials)

therefore:

I am inclined to express my sexual drives and desires by acting

_____

(keywords for sign)

I am inclined to express my anger in a way that will develop

_____

(developmental potentials)

therefore:

I am inclined to express anger by acting

_____

(keywords for sign)

I am inclined to be assertive in a way that will develop

_____

(developmental potentials)

therefore:

I am inclined to be assertive by acting

_____

(keywords for sign)

Additional Sentences
For Your Mars Sign Position

I am inclined to express my sexual drives and desires by focusing on activities that will develop

_____

(developmental potentials)

therefore:

I am inclined to express my sexual drives and desires by focusing on

_____

(keywords for house)

I am inclined to express my anger by focusing on activities that will develop

_____

(developmental potentials)

therefore:

I am inclined to express anger by focusing on

_____

(keywords for house)

I am inclined to be assertive by focusing on activities that will develop

_____

(developmental potentials)

therefore:

I am inclined to be assertive by focusing on

_____

(keywords for house)

Additional Sentences For Your Jupiter Sign

I am inclined to seek ideas for my belief system in a way that will develop

_____

(developmental potentials)

therefore:

I am inclined to seek ideas for my belief system by acting

_____

(keywords for sign)

I am inclined to explore new horizons in a way that will develop

_____

(developmental potentials)

therefore:

I am inclined to explore new horizons by acting

_____

(keywords for sign)

I am inclined to expand beyond my circumstances in life in a way that will develop

_____

(developmental potentials)

therefore:

I am inclined to expand beyond my circumstances in life by acting

_____

(keywords for sign)

Additional Sentences
For Your Jupiter House Position

I am inclined to seek ideas for my belief system by focusing on activities that will develop

_____

(developmental potentials)

therefore:

I am inclined to seek ideas for my belief system by focusing on

_____

(keywords for house)

I am inclined to explore new horizons by focusing on activities that will develop

_____

(developmental potentials)

therefore:

I am inclined to explore new horizons by focusing on

_____

(keywords for house)

I am inclined to expand beyond my circumstances in life by focusing on activities that will develop

_____

(developmental potentials)

therefore:

I am inclined to expand beyond my circumstances in life by focusing on

_____

(keywords for house)

Additional Sentences For Your Saturn Sign

I am inclined to organize and structure life in a way that will develop

_____

(developmental potentials)

therefore:

I am inclined to organize and structure life by acting

_____

(keywords for sign)

I am inclined to handle self-doubt from others' judgment in a way that will develop

_____

(developmental potentials)

therefore:

I am inclined to handle self-doubt from others' judgment by acting

_____

(keywords for sign)

I am inclined to be responsible and self-disciplined in a way that will develop

_____

(developmental potentials)

therefore:

I am inclined to be responsible and self-disciplined by acting

_____

(keywords for sign)

Additional Sentences
For Your Saturn House Position

I am inclined to organize and structure life by focusing on activities that will develop

_____

(developmental potentials)

therefore:

I am inclined to organize and structure life by focusing on

_____

(keywords for house)

I am inclined to handle self-doubt from others' judgment by focusing on activities that will develop

_____

(developmental potentials)

therefore:

I am inclined to handle self-doubt from others' judgment by focusing on

_____

(keywords for house)

I am inclined to be responsible and self-disciplined by focusing on activities that will develop

_____

(developmental potentials)

therefore:

I am inclined to be responsible and self-disciplined by focusing on

_____

(keywords for house)

Additional Sentences For Your Uranus Sign

I am inclined to use my intuitive perceptions of future possibilities in a way that will develop

_____

(developmental potentials)

therefore:

I am inclined to use my intuitive perceptions of future possibilities by acting

_____

(keywords for sign)

I am inclined to change outdated ideas and expectations in a way that will develop

_____

(developmental potentials)

therefore:

I am inclined to change outdated ideas and expectations by acting

_____

(keywords for sign)

I am inclined to use my higher, inventive mind in a way that will develop

_____

(developmental potentials)

therefore:

I am inclined to use my higher, inventive mind by acting

_____

(keywords for house)

Additional Sentences
For Your Uranus House Position

I am inclined to use my intuitive perceptions of future possibilities by focusing on activities that will develop

_____

(developmental potentials)

therefore:

I am inclined to use my intuitive perceptions of future possibilities by focusing on

_____

(keywords for house)

I am inclined to change outdated ideas and expectations by focusing on activities that will develop

_____

(developmental potentials)

therefore:

I am inclined to change outdated ideas and expectations by focusing on

_____

(keywords for house)

I am inclined to use my higher, inventive mind by focusing on activities that will develop

_____

(developmental potentials)

therefore:

I am inclined to use my higher, inventive mind by focusing on

_____

(keywords for house)

Additional Sentences For Your Neptune Sign

I am inclined to express my feelings of universal oneness, compassion and empathy in a way that will develop

_____

(developmental potentials)

therefore:

I am inclined to express my feelings of universal oneness, compassion and empathy by acting

_____

(keywords for sign)

I am inclined to be open to other dimensions and alternate realities in a way that will develop

_____

(developmental potentials)

therefore:

I am inclined to be open to other dimensions and alternate realities by acting

_____

(keywords for sign)

I am inclined to use my higher, universal emotional nature in a way that will develop

_____

(developmental potentials)

therefore:

I am inclined to use my higher, universal emotional nature by acting

_____

(keywords for sign)

Additional Sentences
For Your Neptune House Position

I am inclined to express my feelings of universal oneness, compassion and empathy by focusing on activities that will develop

_____

(developmental potentials)

therefore:

I am inclined to express my feelings of universal oneness, compassion and empathy by focusing on

_____

(keywords for house)

I am inclined to be open to other dimensions and alternate realities by focusing on activities that will develop

_____

(developmental potentials)

therefore:

I am inclined to be open to other dimensions and alternate realities by focusing on

_____

(keywords for house)

I am inclined to use my higher, universal emotional nature by focusing on activities that will develop

_____

(developmental potentials)

therefore:

I am inclined to use my higher, universal emotional nature by focusing on

_____

(keywords for house)

Additional Sentences For Your Pluto Sign

I am inclined to consciously face and integrate the "dark" unaccepted sides of myself in a way that will develop

_____

(developmental potentials)

therefore:

I am inclined to consciously face and integrate the "dark" unaccepted sides of myself by acting

_____

(keywords for sign)

I am inclined to passionately lose myself in a loving relationship in a way that will develop

_____

(developmental potentials)

therefore:

I am inclined to passionately lose myself in a loving relationship by acting

_____

(keywords for sign)

I am inclined to use my capacity for psychological transformation in a way that will develop

_____

(developmental potentials)

therefore:

I am inclined to use my capacity for psychological transformation by acting

_____

(keywords for sign)

Additional Sentences
For Your Pluto House Position

I am inclined to consciously face and integrate the "dark" unaccepted sides of myself by focusing on activities that will develop

_____

(developmental potentials)

therefore:

I am inclined to consciously face and integrate the "dark" unaccepted sides of myself by focusing on

_____

(keywords for house)

I am inclined to passionately lose myself in a loving relationship by focusing on activities that will develop

_____

(developmental potentials)

therefore:

I am inclined to passionately lose myself in a loving relationship by focusing on

_____

(keywords for house)

I am inclined to use my capacity for psychological transformation by focusing on activities that will develop

_____

(developmental potentials)

therefore:

I am inclined to use my capacity for psychological transformation by focusing on

_____

(keywords for signs)

Appendix VI
Sign/House Developmental Potentials and Keywords For Sentence Completion Exercises

Aries/1st House

Developmental Potentials

- my self-identity.

- my sense of personal freedom and independence.

- my ability to project myself assertively into the environment.

- my enthusiasm about life, myself and my needs.

- my ability to live in the present moment.

- my ability to think optimistically of each moment as a possible new beginning.

- my ability to act forcefully in my own behalf and in order to get what I want when I need it.

- my ability to use my personal energy powerfully and purposely.

1st House - Focuses Of Activity

The forceful use of my personal energy

My personal freedoms and desires

Acting spontaneously in each moment

Projecting myself strongly to others

My self-image

My appearance to others

My persona (mask)

My self-discoveries

Developing my self-identity

My unique approach to life

Finding who I am

Taking the initiative in activities

Initiating others into action

Starting new directions in life

Self-centered interests

Positive Development

Assertively
Forcefully
Actively
Spontaneously
Freely
Energetically
Optimistically
Innovatively
With inspiration
Initiatingly
Eagerly
Freshly
Independently
Speedily
With fast starts
With a strong projection of self
Instinctively
Willfully
Urgently
Bravely
Daringly
Innocently
With one direction in mind
With a need to start new things

Lack Of Or Over Development

With difficulty finishing what one starts
Aggressively
Impetuously
Impulsively
Recklessly
Rashly
Wildly
Abrasively
Without considering the consequences
Without considering others' needs
Overbearingly
Combatively

Taurus/2nd House

Developmental Potentials

- my self-reliance.

- my sense of self-worth.

- my ability to meet my basic survival needs in order to be secure and safe in the physical world.

- my ability to be steadfast, unchangeable and determined on my own behalf.

- my sensuality for pleasurable and artistic pursuits.

- my ability to establish my personal resources and obtain the possessions that I need.

- my ability to give physical form to my personal energy.

- my awareness of the concrete, physical realities of life.

2nd House - Focuses Of Activity

My financial needs and resources

Self-reliance

My sensuality

My basic survival needs

My personal, physical and material resources

My earning and spending habits

My possessions and physical attachments

My values toward personal wealth

Self-worth

Productivity

Personal business pursuits

Sensual artistic sensitivities

Enjoying the physical world

Sensual appetites and pleasures

Money

Commerce

Positive Development

Self-reliantly
Sensually
Resourcefully
Productively
Steadfastly
Dependably
Groundedly
Concretely
Solidly
With financial stability
With a need for sensual pleasure
Enduringly
With stability
Practically
Cautiously
With a need to provide for oneself
Patiently
Artistically
Reliably
With rock-like dependability
Consolodatingly
Luxuriously
Deliberately
Retentively
Unchangingly

Lack Of Or Over Development

Fixedly
Cautiously
Possessively
Stubbornly
With inertia
Self-indulgently
Materialistically
Lazily
Unyieldingly
Slowly

Gemini/3rd House

Developmental Potentials

- my ability to learn and to think rationally.

- my personal thinking patterns and style.

- my rational, logical mental nature.

- my self-education.

- my ability to make connections and coordinate my ideas and myself in my personal environment.

- my mental flexibility and versatility.

- my ability to coordinate my physical movement.

- my dexterity and agility.

- my ability to communicate my ideas to others.

- my speaking and writing abilities.

Positive Development

Rationally
Persuasively
Verbally
Talkatively
Quickly
Connectively
Fluently
Cleverly
Mercurially
Whimsically
Adaptably
Communicatively
Inquisitively
With a healthy curiosity
Mentally perceptive
Intellectually
Synthesizingly
Logically
Convincingly
With a need for variety
With a need to do many things at once
With agility
With mental and manual dexterity
With versatility
With wit

3rd House - Focuses Of Activity

My thinking style and habits

Rational perceptions

Mental and physical coordination

My personal communications

Self-education

Learning and teaching concrete information and facts

Logical, rational thinking

Synthesizing information

Reading and writing about personal concerns

Reading books, magazines, journals

Day-to-day environment

Establishing immediate connections in everyday environment

My private thoughts

Experiencing variety in life

Short trips near my home

The use of rational mind

Verbally persuading and convincing others (discussing, debating

Using communication equipment (telephone, faxes, etc.)

Networking

My dexterity and agility

Lack Of Or Over Development

Superficially
With scatteredness
In a shallow manner
Nervously
Inconsistently
Too rationally
Too talkatively
Flightily
Frivolously
Capriciously

Cancer/4th House

Developmental Potentials

- my personal sense of emotional security.

- my ability to get in touch with and to satisfy my personal emotional needs.

- my ability to feel good about myself.

- my capacity for self-love, self-acceptance and self-nurturance.

- my ability to create a comfortable, secure environment where I can most be myself.

- my individualistic emotional focus and clarity.

- my awareness of my instinctive, subjective motivations.

- my personal imagination.

- my ability to draw from my past attachments and memories in order to build my own emotional, internal structures and securities.

4th House - Focuses Of Activity

Personal emotional needs

Emotional security

Emotional nurturing of self and others (especially children)

Emotional comfort

Feeling good about myself

Personal psychological awareness

Personal emotional focus and clarity

Coping emotionally with life

Domestic (household) affairs and comfort

My psychological homebase or place of security

My emotional security and stability

My personal emotional boundaries

My inner motivations

What emotionally satisfies myself

My private self (introversion)

Family, tradition, roots of being

My subconscious

Early childhood environmental influences (emotional conditioning)

Special memories of the past

♋ CANCER
Ways Of Acting

Positive Development

Nuturingly

With unconditional love

With a sense of emotional wholeness

With emotional clarity

Responsively

Sensitively

Caringly

Subjectively

With a need for emotional security

To create a secure homebase

To satisfy my emotional needs

To satisfy my family needs

Supportively

With a need to emotionally protect myself

Self-acceptingly

Domestically

Imaginatively

With a need to do what is emotionally satisfying

With a need to hold onto the past

With tenacity

Traditionally

With family loyalty

Sympathetically

Lack Of Or Over Development

With subconscious emotional blocks

With a tendency to easily feel hurt

Insecurely

Defensively

Clingingly

With emotional dependency

Shyly

Fearfully

Crankily

Moodily

Leo/5th House

Developmental Potentials

- my ability to express my emotions and love nature to others in a warm, confident manner.

- my ability to lead others.

- my personal, unique creativity.

- my recognition of the importance of expression and creativity for its own sake.

- my ability to enjoy myself and relax.

- my ability to relate to the drama and romance of life.

- my ability to actualize my individual potentials.

- my ability for remaining psychologically centered through life's changing circumstances.

Positive Development

Creatively
Self-expressively
Confidently
Dramatically
Charismatically
With leadership confidence
Appealingly
Impressively
Influentially
Self-assuredly
Vitally
Radiantly
Warmly
Extrovertedly
Entertainingly
Theatrically
With a need for attention
Royally
With a need to perform
Pleasurably
Leisurely
Playfully
Flamboyantly
Cavalierly
Romantically

Lack Of Or Over Development

Egotistically
Domineeringly
Conceitedly
With a need to be served by others
Self-centeredly
Childishly
Arrogantly
Narcissistically
Snobbishly
Pompously

5th House - Focuses Of Activity

Confident self-expression

My individual creativity

Externalizing my emotions in a confident manner

Being the center of attention

Being a leader

Romantic adventures

Courtship and love as the giving and getting of special attention

Relating to my inner child

Leisure

Playing and relaxing

Recreation, games, sports

The creative process more than the end results

Entertainment, drama, theater, the performing arts

Acting upon a stage (in life or in the theater)

Virgo/6th House

Developmental Potentials

- my ability to work daily at improving myself and my self-expression.

- my analytical, mental nature so that I can solve problems and difficulties.

- my efficiency and skills.

- my ability to heal myself physically through consistent effort and discipline.

- my ability to notice the details of life in order to identify the imperfections that need improvement.

- my ability to help and serve others in personal ways.

- my ability to make the necessary adjustments and fine tuning that make life run more smoothly.

6th House - Focuses Of Activity

Improving my self-expression

Rational problem solving

Mental analysis and efficiency

Skills and craftsmanship

Serving and helping others

The fine tuning that makes life run more smoothly

Noticing and correcting mistakes and faults

Making mental and physical adjustments to solve personal crisis and sickness

Health, nutrition, physical therapy

Routine and work

Following daily routines

Work habits

Working conditions

Employee concerns

Physical and mental labor

Neatness

Physical healing and rehabilitation

Positive Development

Efficiently
Precisely
In A Serving Manner
Analytically
Helpfully
Self-improvingly
Skillfully
Usefully
Industriously
Routinely
With a need to improve oneself physically
With a concern about details
Neatly
With a concern about health
Exactly
With the proper use of techniques
To mentally solve problems
Methodically
Thoroughly
Modestly
Discriminatingly
Humbly
Unassumingly
Diligently
To Work Hard
Dutifully

Lack Of Or Over Development

Too critically
With too much concern about details
Perfectionistically
Uptightly
Worringly
Complainingly
Puritanically
With pettiness
Nit-pickingly
Fault-finding

Libra/7th House

Developmental Potentials

Sociably

Cooperatively

Aesthetically

Harmonizingly

Diplomatically

With Social charm

With Social ease

With fairness

Impartially

With an ability to listen fully to others

With others' needs in mind

With social poise

Gracefully

Beautifully

Elegantly

With inner balance

With a need to create social harmony

Mediatingly

With equality

Agreeably

Objectively

Even-mindedly

With a need to please others

Affectionately

With ideals about love

Conventionally

- my ability to be receptive of other's needs

- my ability to achieve a sense of inner balance and harmony.

- my sense of social awareness.

- my receptivity to other's needs.

- my ability to be receptive to other people who can help complete what I feel lacking in myself.

- my ability to feel comfortable and satisfied in social situations.

- my sense of fair play between two individuals.

- my intellectual, objective consideration of opposite viewpoints.

- my ability to gracefully relate to others.

- my aesthetic nature.

7th House - Focuses Of Activity

My social relationships

My social awareness

Significant others in my life

Establishing important relationships

Creating social harmony

Using interpersonal communication skills

One-to-one encounters

Cooperating with others

Seeing both sides of an issue

My sense of balance an symmetry

Seeking completion in others

My ideals in aesthetics and beauty

My ideals in love and relationships

Finding a mate

Partnerships in business or marriage

Projections onto others

Conventional social expectations

Social gracefulness and charm

Etiquette

Lack Of Or Over Development

Compromisingly

Superficially

Competitively

Manipulatively

Indecisively

Vacillatingly

With too much of a need to please others

With a difficulty being alone

With love too much in my mind, not in my heart

Scorpio/8th House

Developmental Potentials

- my ability to be an emotionally sharing individual.

- my ability to allow my ego to be transformed through emotional interactions with others.

- my sexuality as a loving and regenerating act

- my emotional control of selfish desires in order to transform them into loving actions.

- my ability to transform and release pent-up, repressed emotions in positive creative expressions.

- my ability to understand the deepest emotions of others

- my ability to involve myself in mutually transforming relationships.

- my ability to dissolve the emotional separation between myself and someone else.

- my ability to lose a sense of individual separateness through total involvement with another person.

8th House - Focuses Of Activity

Intense emotional interaction and sharing

Intimacy

Sexual interaction as a process of emotional sharing and loving

Discovering hidden emotions in self and others

Emotional power, strength and control

Sharing resources

Interdependency

Losing my sense of separateness in a relationship

Fruitfulness of a relationship (self-transformation money, growth)

Deeply felt, peak experiences through social rituals

Regeneration or repression of emotions

Psychotherapy (psychological transformation)

Emotional risk-taking

Karma from past relationships (debts)

Emotional obsessions

♏ SCORPIO Ways Of Acting

Positive Development

With emotional depth
Magnetically
Interdependently
Psychologically
With emotional intensity
To bond emotionally with someone else
Intimately
Passionately
Sexually
Erotically
Seductively
Provocatively
To lose my sense of separateness
To fully satisfy my sexual partner
Fervently
With emotional concentration
Penetratingly
Probingly
With emotional control
Interpersonally
Jointly
Transformingly
Cathartically
With a need to elevate my selfish desires
With emotional commitment

Lack Of Or Over Development

With emotional rigidity
With difficulty expressing my emotions
Secretively
With an inner emotional power struggle
Sarcastically
Revengefully
Obsessively
With emotional possessiveness
Repressively
Resentfully

Sagittarius/9th House

Developmental Potentials

- my ability to expand myself into new social community and spiritual realms.

- my ability to see the opportunities in life to become more than I am.

- my ability to expand my mental horizons and to think abstractly.

- my ability to see the underlying patterns in life.

- my belief system and principles of life based on personal experiences.

- my long range vision and understanding.

- my ability to search for meaning, truth and ideals and exchange them with others.

- my ability to learn from others and teach others about the deeper meanings of existence.

- my ability to travel far and wide physically and in my mind.

- my ability to see the humor in the exaggerations of life.

Positive Development

Expansively
Enthusiastically
Knowledgeably
Adventurously
Searchingly
To broaden my understanding of life
To find and take advantage of life's opportunities
Comprehensively
Abstractly
Philosophically
With a need to share ideas with others
Idealistically
With a need for long distance travel
Humorously
Jovially
Academically
Morally
Religiously
Zealously
With a need to gain wisdom through experience
With a need to explore new horizons
With far-reaching thoughts
With wide-ranging ideas
With candid honesty
Truthfully

Lack Of Or Over Development

Excessively
Exceedingly
Irresponsibly
Extravagantly
Dogmatically
Fanatically
With mental intolerance
Insensitively
With a tendency to preach
With a tendency to overextend myself

9th House - Focuses Of Activity

Opportunities for growth

The search for meaning and truth

Exchanging truth and knowledge with others

A quest for knowledge

Learning and teaching abstract ideas and concepts

Higher education

Exploring new mental, physical horizons

Broadening my understanding of my self and of life

Expanding my realms of social interaction and influence

Establishing my principles and beliefs to live by

Living according to my beliefs

Long-distance travel

Spiritual apprenticeship and/or teaching

Capricorn/10th House

Developmental Potentials

- my sense of social limits and responsibility.

- my ability to achieve effective organization and order.

- my ability to work patiently and with perseverance toward the attainment of a goal.

- my ability to build toward the achievement of my life aims in a way that will be accepted by others.

- my reputation and my community, public position.

- my ability to meet the expectations of the society that I live in.

- my ability to build constructive, dependable, yet resilient structures.

- my ability to regulate self with a sense of patience and timing.

- my ability to discipline myself with realistic demands.

- my ability to gain maturity by meeting the tests and challenges in life.

10th House - Focuses Of Activity

My responsibility to the community

My professional reputation

My community power

My career achievement

Establishing and maintaining order

My self-discipline

My self-control and self-regulation

Living up to external standards and expectations

Community restriction and obligation

Career stability and foundation

Authority and authority figures

Conservatism

Patience and perseverance

My community aims and goals

Finishing what is started

Sustained efforts

Achieving mastery over the physical world

Building physical structures

Accountability to society

Positive Development

With Organization
Responsibly
Orderly
Constructively
Realistically
To set realistic limits
To achieve career goals
With sustained effort
To meet up to high standards
With practical wisdom
Reputably
With self-discipline
With self-control
With a sense of timing
With a need to finish what starts
Perserveringly
With concentration
Maturely
Authoritatively
With structure
With a need for prestige
With a need to be professional
Pragmatically
Within limits
Traditionally

Lack Of Or Over Development

With inhibition
Guiltily
Rigidly
Bureaucratically
Pessimistically
Self-condemningly
Judgementally
Constrictively
With self-doubt
Austerely
Sternly

Aquarius/11th House

Developmental Potentials

Inventively
With social concerns
Experimentally
Multi-culturally
Progressively
Ingeniously
To break free from unfair restrictions
Experimentally
To find a new, better ways of doing things
Altruistically
Humanistically
With a need for liberation
With original ideas
Holistically
Intuitively
With a need to give everyone special & equal attention
With a need to exist within groups
Originally
Independently
Futuristically
Liberally
Unconventionally
Idealistically
Democratically

- my ability to get in touch with my intuitive universal mental nature

- my ability to mentally perceive beyond the limits of space and time or linear thinking

- my progressive, futuristic, inventive thinking patterns

- my ability to help make the world a better place to live.

- my ability to urge society to serve the needs of the individual.

- my ability to break free from, and shatter social structures and influences that are too rigid or out-dated

- my ability to perceive the oneness of all humanity

- the understanding that my individuality can be a channel for universal creativity and the evolution of humanity

11th House - Focuses Of Activity

The community's responsibility to individual rights and freedoms

Creative, symbolic expression on mental levels (scientifically and artistically)

Futuristic, inventive thinking

Experimenting (scientifically, artistically, socially, etc.)

Social causes, issues, ideals, progress reform

Total openness and acceptance to all living beings

Multicultural, international interests

Humanitarian concerns

Being a channel for group expression and creativity

Common links to others beyond space and time

Mass communication

Breaking away from rigid outdated ways of doing things

Mental openness to infinite universal sources of wisdom and insight

Mentally transcending the limits of time-space reality, sexual gender, personal background, cultural conditioning & societal expectation

Lack Of Or Over Development
Eccentrically
Erratically
Coolly
Anti-socially
Rebelliously
Unexpectedly
Remotely
Emotionally detached
With too fixed ideas
Unpredictably

Pisces/12th House

Developmental Potentials

- my universal emotional nature

- my ability to get in touch with my collective unconscious and universal realities through dreams, meditations and visualizations

- my sense of universal imagination, beauty and aesthetics

- my ability to be empathetic and compassionate, and to give without concern for receiving back

- my ability to merge myself with the oneness of the universe through spiritual pursuits

- my ability to surrender myself to the unknown and accept the chaos and formlessness of universal realities

- my ability to dissolve my ego concerns and attachments to past successes and failures in order to experience a rebirth into new directions

12th House - Focuses Of Activity

Inner spiritual realities

Transcendental, psychic receptivity

Universal love, beauty, harmony, imagination

Visions, fantasies, dreams

Inner realities, universal impressions

Solitude

Using dreams as a source of wisdom and guidance

Getting in touch with my universally refined inner qualities

Freeing myself from psychological repressions

Emotionally transcending the limits of time-space reality, sexual gender, personal background, cultural conditioning, and social expectation

Coming to terms and transcending the "ghosts of the past"

Overcoming the fear of the unknown and of chaos

Empathizing with the suffering of others

Becoming aware of the unconscious sides of self

Mysticism

Psychological escapism and addiction

Deception

Spiritual retreat

Positive Development

Compassionately
Empathetically
Spiritually
Psychically
With emotional wisdom
Imaginatively
With receptivity to universal visions and images
With a rich inner dream world
Transcendently
Subtly
Selflessly
With highly refined emotional perceptions
Ethereally
Impressionably
Peacefully
Sacrificially
Romantically
Mysteriously
Formlessly
Intangibly
Magically
Dreamily
Gently
Kindly
Poetically
Glamorously

Lack Of Or Over Development

Unconsciously
Confusedly
Moodily
Deceptively
Indiscriminately
Hypersensitivity
Addictively
Passively
Unrealistically
Evasively